KITCHENS
THAT WORK

KITCHENS
THAT WORK

Martin Edic and Richard Edic

The Taunton Press

PUBLISHER: James P. Chiavelli
ACQUISITIONS EDITOR: Rick Peters
PUBLISHING COORDINATOR: Joanne Renna
EDITOR: Jennifer Renjilian
DESIGNERS: Barbara Sudick, Jodie Delohery
LAYOUT ARTIST: Ken Swain
PHOTOGRAPHERS, EXCEPT WHERE NOTED: David Mohney
    and Richard Edic
ILLUSTRATOR: Michael Gellatly

FRONT COVER PHOTO: Jonathan Binzen,
    © The Taunton Press, Inc.; kitchen designed
    by MORIMOTO ARCHITECTS, Berkeley, California

 **The Taunton Press**
Inspiration for hands-on living®

Printed in the United States of America
10 9 8 7 6

Kitchens That Work was originally published in hardcover
© 1997 by The Taunton Press, Inc.

The Taunton Press
63 South Main Street
PO Box 5506
Newtown, CT 06470-5506
e-mail: tp@taunton.com

Library of Congress Cataloging-in-Publication Data

Edic, Martin.
    Kitchens that work / Martin Edic and Richard Edic.
        p.   cm.
    ISBN-13: 978-1-56158-177-1 hardcover
    ISBN-10: 1-56158-177-1 hardcover
    ISBN-13: 978-1-56158-319-5 softcover
    ISBN 1-56158-319-7 softcover
    1. Kitchens—Planning.   2. Kitchens—Design and construction.
    3. Kitchens—Remodeling.   I. Edic, Richard.   II. Title.
    TX655.E35   1997   97-9293
    643'.3—dc21   CIP

Acknowledgments

This book would not have been possible without the support and encouragement of many people. Special thanks to the families that welcomed us into their homes to photograph their kitchens. Your patience and creativity were an inspiration. Thanks also to Richard Reisem, Joanna Guglielmino, Jon Schick, Tom Bradshaw, Rob Salerno, and our wives, Jane Hasselkus and Annie Wells. Rick Peters, Jim Chiavelli, Joanne Renna, and the entire crew at Taunton have been a pleasure to work with. In particular, we'd like to thank Jennifer Renjilian for both her editing skills and the patience she showed two anxious authors throughout the development of this book. Finally, thanks to our photographer and good friend, Dave Mohney, for his help, relaxed attitude, and talent.

Contents

Introduction

Of all the rooms in our homes, the kitchen is the most complex. Designing one that works well and lives well is a challenge. This book was written to help you create a kitchen that works with you in the context of your life and the lifestyle of your household. Too many of the kitchens we use daily work against us, making regular tasks tedious and extraordinary tasks like entertaining a chore rather than a pleasure. We all spend a lot of time in the kitchen even if we never cook a gourmet meal. We eat there, we socialize, we work, we organize, and we recharge our engines for another challenging day.

Kitchens That Work is a book about the design process. Every time we design and build a kitchen for someone we go through an educational process with our clients, as they learn about everything from hidden heating ducts in the ceilings to making sure that their counter edges are safe for small children. Kitchens are not only the social heart of the house, but they are also often the utilitarian heart of the house, the place where all the life-support systems we depend on converge. Consider that they should be aesthetically pleasing and functional, too, and you have a design challenge that can stump even the most experienced designer.

We'll be looking at everything from style to plumbing to dealing with contractors. You can use the book to help you communicate your wishes to a professional designer or contractor, or you can use it to guide you through your own design process. We won't tell you how to hook up a dishwasher or build a cabinet because there are plenty of excellent sources for that information. We will help you decide where that dishwasher goes and what the difference is between face-frame and Euro-style cabinetry so that you can make informed choices. Making those choices is what this book is about.

Part 1 of *Kitchens That Work* focuses on the knowledge you already possess. We'll examine how you use your kitchen, what works and what doesn't, and why. We'll look at money and budgets and ways you can get the most from your dollars. Then we'll examine the existing systems and architecture and help you learn how they can be adapted or changed to improve the basic space. Photos, illustrations, and checklists will get you started learning more about the design process as it affects your needs and interests.

Part 2 is about design and style. The design of your kitchen starts with the three-dimensional space and how it flows as a work and social environment. We'll tell you how to plan on paper and build a design file. We'll look again at systems, this time from a design point of view. And we'll look in detail at appliances, cabinetry, and materials, along with how they all work together to create a functional and attractive kitchen. We'll also examine the influence of architecture and explore ways to create a coordinated color and texture palette you can use to choose everything from a counter surface to a cabinet finish.

Part 3 looks at the construction process you'll go through while building a new kitchen. This is often the most stressful aspect of the kitchen-design process, in large part because of poor planning, confusion as to what's going on, and the large sums of money involved. We'll walk you through scheduling, dealing with contractors, buying materials, resolving problems, and putting your new kitchen together again after the dust settles.

We suggest you first use *Kitchens That Work* as a source of inspiration. Look through it and start to consider what you have to work with and what you want from your new kitchen. Then read more thoroughly and start measuring, sketching, and planning. Get out and start looking at the many choices you have in materials, cabinetry, and appliances. Start a design file filled with clippings, samples, and ideas. Consider using a reference model like the ones in Chapter 10 to help you make decisions. Once you have a design and know what you want, use Part 3 to help you get started with the construction of your new kitchen.

If you don't feel up to designing your own kitchen, this book will help you choose and work with a professional kitchen designer or architect. The more informed you are, the better communication you'll have with design professionals, and the more likely you'll be to get what you want. And if you are a designer, we hope you'll share this book with your clients as a tool and inspiration.

We wrote this book because we are fascinated and challenged by kitchen design. Both of us are avid cooks who enjoy entertaining. We've never been able to keep our guests out of the kitchen, nor would we want to. After all, it's where the action is, where the food and drink flow, and where the conversation is the best. We hope this book will help you create a kitchen that works for you.

Part One

THE
EVOLVING
PLAN

CHAPTER 1

A Kitchen That Works for You

"The place I like best in this world is the kitchen. No matter where it is, no matter what kind, if it's a place where they make food, it's fine with me. Ideally it should be well broken in. Lots of tea towels, dry and immaculate. White tile catching the light (ting! ting!)."

—Banana Yoshimoto, *Kitchen*

Kitchens are the centers and hearts of our homes. While growing up we headed to the kitchen for snacks, to check in after school, and to find out what was happening with the rest of the family. As young adults in our first apartments, we equipped our kitchens from secondhand stores and with hand-me-downs. We might have discovered an interest in cooking or entertaining as we had friends over and socialized surrounded by food. We probably discovered that at a party everyone ends up in the kitchen, no matter how hard you try to move the crowd to other parts of the house. Later on, in our own homes, the kitchen assumed other roles: relaxation center, information depot, a spot for coffee before work, a place to cook for dinner parties, and a storage area for all those wedding-gift appliances and housewares.

Eventually almost everyone starts thinking about ways to improve their kitchen. Perhaps friends or business colleagues remodel or build new homes with that state-of-the-art kitchen you've always dreamed of. Maybe your old inefficient layout, outdated look, and aged appliances don't work as well for you now. Your

lifestyle changes as you change, and the ways you use your kitchen change with it. Children, careers, hobbies, and new technology all affect the way we use our kitchens.

These lifestyle considerations are often the underlying reason for remodeling and building a new kitchen. Yet they are seldom considered during the early planning of a new kitchen. Instead, we tend to focus on cabinet styles, wall colors, appliances, and the many items that are found in every kitchen. All too often a new kitchen project begins and ends with a visit to a cabinet store, resulting in a kitchen plan based on how many cabinets will fit in a space and on that store's flavor of the week in finishes and styles. Design comes in second to salesmanship.

Understanding how kitchens became so complex can help you make the many choices necessary while planning your new kitchen. In less

than 100 years, we've gone from wood cookstoves and kitchens manned by servants to halogen cooktops that heat instantaneously with the touch of a button. We're now an egalitarian society that pitches in, washes the dishes, buys the groceries, and chooses the menu, regardless of gender or income. Because we work in our own kitchens, we often have strong opinions about how they are put together.

The Evolution of the Modern Kitchen

Until the 1920s, most kitchens were inefficiently laid out. Families that could afford cooks had large storage pantries removed from the cooking area. With servants doing the work, there was little attempt made to provide convenience and comfort for the homeowner. In poorer households, the kitchen was a corner of the living area, which often resembled a basement sink area more than it resembled our idea of a kitchen (see the photo on the facing page).

In the '20s and '30s, a new kitchen design emerged based on the efficiency methods being employed in industrial assembly lines: separate work areas for washing, preparing, storing, and cooking. Unfortunately, the work areas remained on opposing parts of the room, separated by runs of open wall space. The sink might use one wall, the stove another, the pantry would be around the corner, and the ice box would sit near the door for ac-

The state-of-the-art 1920s kitchen provided little useful continuous work space. Reprinted with permission from Homes & Interiors of the 1920s. *©1987 by Lee Valley Tools. All rights reserved.*

cessibility to the iceman's deliveries (see the illustration on the facing page). The cook did a lot of walking.

Many of us grew up with kitchens remodeled or newly built in the late '40s and early '50s as the baby-boomer generation arrived after World War II. New families meant new construction, which resulted in the first suburban tracts of "modern" homes. Modern meant streamlined and efficient, with rows of connected cabinetry, sleek counters, and more usable work space (see the top photo on p. 10). There still wasn't a lot of work space, but it was a vast improvement over the kitchens of the prewar years.

In the '60s and '70s, we saw the beginnings of contemporary kitchen design. Lighting was improved, new kinds of appliances like dishwashers and garbage disposals became customary, and cabinetry had more durable finishes. Counters were made of new laminate designs that featured bright colors and patterns like the infamous "boomerang" pattern many of us grew up with (recently made available again as a retro look). The downside of these kitchens was that they adhered to a design based on the trends of that year or even that month. Orange counters, barn-wood cabinets, supergraphic wall coverings, and bizarre light fixtures often became outdated within a few years of their initial installation.

This brings us to the present. Cooking has become a serious avocation for many people—not just traditional cooking, but cooking that includes techniques from cultures all over the world. Technology is changing constantly, and the kitchen has been the benefactor of many breakthroughs in lighting, communications, appliances, heating and air-conditioning, recycling, and many other systems. Some

kitchens in homes owned by two-income couples without children or by singles are rarely used for anything other than an occasional microwaved meal. Other kitchens are reproductions of restaurant kitchens complete with commercial high-BTU (British thermal unit) ranges and refrigerators.

Understanding what type of kitchen will work for you can be confusing. Your lifestyle is not the same as that of

A massive wall-mounted sink in a turn-of-the-century home. Exposed plumbing and the lack of under-the-sink storage were common.

Modern convenience was the selling point of postwar kitchens. These kitchens featured the first mass-produced appliances designed to be connected by runs of counters and cabinetry. (Photo ©Brian Vanden Brink.)

The key to a good kitchen is to match it to your lifestyle. For some people, that means reserving space to open up a laptop computer or to read the morning paper.

your boss, your siblings, or your neighbors, and your kitchen design may not resemble theirs. Ultimately, if you want a kitchen that truly works for you and your household's needs, you must take a look at how you use your kitchen now. This is the basis of the lifestyle design concept.

Lifestyle Design

The lifestyle design concept is simple: The way you utilize and enjoy your kitchen should guide you through every step of the design process, from mechanical questions to style decisions. If you don't cook often, you don't need a commercial range. An inexpensive cooktop will do for occasional use. If your kids swarm over the kitchen day and night, doing homework, entertaining friends, using the

phone, and helping with dinner, you're going to want a very different kitchen than the executive couple with no children who entertains regularly, often turning their kitchen over to a caterer or professional cook. In all likelihood, your kitchen will reflect some combination of uses based on your family's lifestyle.

Let's take a look at an assortment of kitchens that reflects the specific needs and lifestyles of their owners—working couples, busy families, serious amateur and professional cooks, people who entertain regularly, people who rarely cook, and those who simply want a kitchen they can show off. Your kitchen is likely to be an amalgam of two or more kitchens based on your lifestyle. Integrating the various requirements of these kitchen types is a basic aspect of kitchen design. Looking at the needs of each type will give you

KITCHEN DESIGN QUESTIONNAIRE

These questions are designed to help you start thinking creatively about how you use your existing kitchen and how you'd like to use your new kitchen. The answers will help you set some guidelines for many of the decisions you'll make as you go through the design process. Be realistic while answering the questions, and be sure to get input from everyone in your household who uses the kitchen.

- What is the primary use of your kitchen?

- What major change would you make to the space in your kitchen (larger, smaller, shape, traffic flow, etc.)?

- What percentage of each day do you and/or your family spend in the kitchen?

- How often do you cook?

- How many people will be cooking and/or working in the kitchen at the same time?

- How often do you entertain?

- How many people do you typically entertain at one time?

- What is the most elaborate meal that you've ever cooked?

- What is the most elaborate meal you can imagine yourself cooking?

- What is the single worst thing about your present kitchen?

- What would you change about each of the following:

    - floor?
    - lighting?
    - appliances?
    - counter/work space?
    - storage?
    - traffic flow?

- How hard are you and your family on your kitchen (wear and tear)?

- What would you like to show off in the new kitchen?

- What would you like to hide?

- How much money can you spend?

- If you had to pick a single luxury item for the kitchen, what would it be?

an idea of what is important in each. They may all contain elements that you want and need in your kitchen.

THE WORKING COUPLE'S KITCHEN

The working couple without children is a late 20th-century phenomenon. With both adults holding responsible jobs or running their own businesses, time and organization become vital to their well-being. Simply getting up and out the door each morning, working all day, and finding time to spend together require a different type of personal scheduling than that of one-income families. In the home, the kitchen is often the common meeting spot in the morning and after work, and it's a place to entertain and relax (see the photo on the facing page).

A kitchen designed for this lifestyle has to cope with several challenges. It must be easy to clean and set up for the preparation of quick meals. It also needs a place for the harried owners to settle down for a moment of relaxation over coffee in the morning or a drink during dinner preparation. If they entertain, the kitchen may double as a bar, a buffet, a place for serious cooking, or simply a gathering spot for a few friends. This kitchen will probably have a number of timesaving appliances like a microwave, an espresso machine, a food processor, and other easy-to-use and easy-to-clean tools. Stereo speakers and a TV

This working couple's kitchen features a spot for a quick meal, careful use of available space, and a blend of natural surfaces and light-reflecting glass cabinetry.

This large family-oriented kitchen has many work areas, allowing several cooks to work together.

are likely as well, offering the couple a chance to catch the news or listen to music while cleaning up.

Traffic patterns in a kitchen designed for two people are simpler than those found in a kitchen designed for a family. A couple can make do with narrower aisles or a smaller space. With no children in the house, the pace may be a little slower and the style a little more unconventional. It's likely that the design will be oriented toward a more minimal, cleaner look than the frantic family kitchen constantly hosting new projects for school or play.

Lighting and mood are variable. In the morning, a bright source of natural light can help get the owners up and alert. In the evening, the lighting can vary from bright task lighting to dramatic mood lighting for a party or

just for relaxing. The focus in these kitchens is on instant comfort, ease of use, and the creation of a place to relax and lower stress levels.

THE FAMILY ORGANIZATION CENTER

The family with kids faces a different set of requirements. While parents share that need for rest and relaxation after a busy day, they may find it in another part of the house, be it a study, master bedroom, or sunporch. The kitchen is family central—the place where dinner is prepared, activities organized, homework done, phones answered, and chaos kept under control (see the photo above).

Traffic patterns are important in a kitchen where kids may be running, where every surface (including the

This kitchen, while small and designed for one user, features restaurant-quality appliances and work surfaces dedicated to serious cooking and entertaining.

and to close off areas when someone needs a little quiet. The flow around the kitchen must work around two people sitting at a counter and someone loading a dishwasher.

Safety is particularly important when children are around and must be taken into consideration at the beginning of the design process. Rounded corners, limited access to appliance controls, childproof doors, safe storage for cleaning supplies, and ways to monitor activity in other parts of the house are all examples of design issues that will come up. Durability also becomes an important consideration when buying floors, cabinets, and appliances. The busy family will beat up on its kitchen in ways that a single person or a couple may not.

If you have kids, you know that you're always playing a game of catch-up, particularly when it comes to cleaning and storage. You'll want durable, easy-to-clean surfaces for floors and counters, stove tops without crevices for food to lodge in, a reliable dishwasher, and a sink with a garbage disposal. Recycling is important these days in all kitchens, and the family kitchen may require a large recycling area. You should make your surface choices with the knowledge that you can replace them in a few years as kids get older and (allegedly) neater.

We all have strong memories of the kitchens we grew up in, and the opportunity to create a memorable kitchen should be a rewarding one for any family. At the same time, a busy family will experience the construction and remodeling process as a greater interruption to its lifestyle than a single person who can easily run out for a meal during the mayhem. Scheduling and planning of your kitchen

floor) is a potential spot for spreading out a drawing or book, and where the cook is besieged with special requests yet needs to stay away from the main traffic flow while handling hot food. The way the room connects to other rooms is vital both to avoid jam-ups

project become especially important when working around the needs of a busy family.

THE SERIOUS COOK'S KITCHEN

Gourmet cooking as a hobby and an avocation has become a popular part of modern life. Dozens of magazines, thousands of cookbooks, television channels devoted to food, mail-order catalogs full of restaurant-quality tools, and availability of exotic ingredients have powered our interest in the fine art of cooking. Any serious cook has dreamed of her ultimate kitchen as a superefficient work space and as a personal place to pursue her craft. Restaurant-style ranges, gleaming stainless-steel appliances, maple butcher-block counters, and overhead racks full of copper pans all appeal to the serious cook. When we get the opportunity to create a kitchen that works the way we want, we often crash into the expensive reality of what these commercial kitchen choices mean.

The kitchen designed for the serious cook is not about stainless steel and 15,000-BTU cooktops, although these appliances have their place. It is about efficiency, about the way the cook functions, and about the size and type of meals the cook prepares. A baker may want a dedicated area with its own mixers, stone work surfaces, shoulder-height oven(s), and special storage for the trays, pans, and utensils used in baking (see the photo at right). A vegetarian with an interest in exotic dishes may work out of a wok 90% of the time, while a cook versed in classic French techniques may have an extensive collection of cooking tools, or as the French call it, *la batterie*

de cuisine. Even though the kitchens for specialist cooks may look quite different, they share a need for a functional, well-designed work space.

Layout of the work space is the key to an efficient kitchen for a serious cook, so if you fall into this category, the answers to the following questions

The owner of this kitchen is an avid baker. A former pantry area was converted into a wing of the kitchen devoted to baking, with granite work surfaces, a convection oven, and its own sink.

will be paramount in determining the layout of your kitchen.

- How many people will use the kitchen?
- How many will you typically cook for?
- Do you need large cutting and prep areas?
- Should storage for spices, herbs, and condiments, fresh and dried, be easily accessible?
- Do you want an efficient, easy-to-clean cooktop or a massive six-burner range with its required ventilation and safety systems?
- Do you want a place to display your treasured collection of pots and pans, knives, and tools?
- Do you need a place to keep track of recipes?
- If you entertain, do you want the cooking area hidden from guests, or do you want to be able to socialize at a party instead of cooking in the back?

All of these considerations cost money, take careful planning, and can mean a big difference in your enjoyment of your kitchen. As a serious cook, you'll spend a lot of time in your space, and you'll regret any oversights made during the design process. In later chapters, we'll look at ways you can fit in all of the features you want with the budget you have and still create a kitchen that works well for you.

THE ENTERTAINING COOK'S KITCHEN

Kitchens and entertaining go hand in hand. Guests gravitate toward the kitchen, perhaps drawn by the desire to be closer to the action, whether for an informal conversation over a cup of coffee or for a formal dinner party. For people who entertain frequently, these kitchen gatherings can have a significant effect on the design of the new kitchen. Even if entertaining takes place in the dining room or outdoors, the requirements of preparing meals for groups are different than those for a typical family.

The entertaining cook needs space—counter space, storage space, cooking-surface space, baking space, and room to maneuver prepared food from one space to another. Often the cook will want to interact with guests during preparation, turning the kitchen into a combination of social and work space. In that case, the kitchen may require room for drinks or a bar, for unobtrusive speakers for music, and for an area with some seating, all separated from the busy food-preparation areas. Often an island or peninsula counter can serve as a divider that allows the cook to socialize while preparing and serving food (see the photo on the facing page).

While rare, it is possible that those who entertain large groups often may need to turn the kitchen over to caterers, who bring in prepared food and ready it for serving on the premises, or to professional cooks, who use the kitchen to prepare a custom dinner. These professionals have needs, including easy access from outside, large areas of table or counter space for prepping food, and a cleanup area that can handle large pans, trays, and quantities of dishes. The pathways from prep to dining areas need to be easy to traverse with serving dishes while the areas themselves need to be separate enough to keep noise down. All of these considerations must be dealt with at the beginning of the design process.

If your entertaining style is more casual and involves smaller, more intimate groups, you won't need as much space, but you will find that the more space you plan for up front, the more enjoyable your kitchen will be when cooking for others. In addition to space requirements, many of the needs of the serious cook detailed on pp. 15-16 also apply to an entertaining cook.

THE UTILITY KITCHEN

With the advent of take-out, fast food, deliveries from restaurants, and pre-prepared food from the grocery store, fewer and fewer people are actually cooking in their kitchens. Many people who have no interest in or time for elaborate cooking use their kitchens as utilitarian storage and simple prep spaces, using the microwave, coffee-maker, and refrigerator more than the chef's knife or food processor. It makes a lot of sense for these utility kitchens to be designed to facilitate these simple needs.

The characteristics of a utility kitchen are: a simple design; labor-saving appliances; a floor plan that makes it easy to sit down and watch the news, listen to music, or work while waiting for a meal; and surfaces that are easy to clean with a quick pass of a sponge. Basic cooktops, refrigerators with built-in hot and cold water taps and ice makers, built-in microwaves and small electric convection ovens, espresso machines, and other easy-to-use appliances are better choices than large, complex, professional-quality types.

If you're planning a utility kitchen, consider those rare times when you might want to entertain, even if you're bringing in a meal and heating

This layout keeps the busy cook in the thick of things when entertaining. The wall of glass doors looking out on a large deck also integrates cooking and outdoor social activities.

it up. Also, it's typical for the needs of noncooks to change as they get older, so you may want to consider how you'd make the transition to a more functional kitchen in the future. Style may lean toward the "form follows function" school more than the big design statement. As with any kitchen, the ultimate style should be determined by your lifestyle.

THE KITCHEN AS A SHOWPLACE

A new kitchen is often the focal point of the house, and it can be tempting to go all out and create a showplace featuring the latest design trends, expensive cabinetry, and a high level of craftsmanship. In fact, it's not unusual for such a kitchen to be built primarily to make a big impression. While creating a showplace kitchen can be an intriguing project, it's important to stick to good design principles and functional layouts even if you rarely prepare big meals. Inevitably, even casual kitchen users become a lot more involved in cooking and entertaining as a result of building a showplace kitchen, so it's important to make sure the style and design are more than skin deep.

The issue of style brings up choices and decisions that can be extremely challenging. Visualizing colors, textures, lighting, and use of space in three dimensions are skills that take professionals years to develop. It is tempting to choose an attractive trend

It helps to visualize your space as a blank canvas. The owners of this kitchen outlined the new layout on the floor to help them see how it will work in reality.

and follow it slavishly. The often unfortunate results are kitchen designs that look like wallpaper showrooms, cabinetry catalogs, or the latest trend, which can become dated before the paint dries. Classic design that holds up over time starts with function and architecture, considers ambience and comfort levels, and uses the best materials in an understated, well-crafted manner.

The Perfect-World Kitchen

When imagining your ideal kitchen, start with a perfect-world viewpoint—imagine the kitchen you would want in a perfect world. It's a good way to start off the design process. Develop a picture in your head of all the things your ideal kitchen would have if you

were unencumbered by concerns about money, space, or time. List everything you'd want, clip pictures from magazines, and make sketches.

The reasoning behind the perfect-world kitchen is simple: You'll find out what is really important to you without automatically eliminating certain things because of price or other considerations. Often you'll find that there is a way to make those important aspects of your perfect-world kitchen happen within your real world. If you start out by eliminating them, you may never know how easy it might have been to fit them in.

Another benefit of the perfect-world process is that you'll find out that some fantasy items aren't really very important when you start to think seriously about them. You'll be able to assess their importance at the beginning, and you may discover that you can eliminate them without losing your original vision. This can clear the way for those granite countertops that you'd previously decided you couldn't afford. In Part 2, we'll give you a model for an effective way to start the design process. For now, give yourself permission to create a perfect-world kitchen. The process starts with the following statement: In a perfect world, my kitchen would…. You fill in the blanks. (See the sample list at right.)

SAMPLE PERFECT-WORLD KITCHEN LIST

A no-holds-barred perfect-world kitchen list will help you define what is important in your kitchen. Your list may be very different from the example here, but both can help identify important aspects of a dream kitchen that can become a reality.

- Unlimited space in floor plan

- Access to extensive vegetable and herb garden, patio area, garage, adjoining living space, and outdoor kitchen

- Blend of general, task, and accent lighting with variable controls

- Integrated music, TV/video, CD-ROM/computer, and intercom systems

- Large counter areas in each designated work center

- Open areas with bar seating and couch/lounge, socializing space next to work space, and semiconcealed areas for cleanup and prep work

- Storage for every imaginable piece of kitchen equipment, food, linens, computer, cleaning supplies, and recycling bins

- Display areas for prized possessions

- Combination of incredibly stylish look with total functionality (ease of use and cleanup)

- Finest materials available: granite countertops, handmade German sinks, full-size restaurant stove, custom-made cabinetry with exotic hardwoods and fine finishes, tile or stone floors, state-of-the-art appliances, etc.

From Perfect World to Real World

Once you've spent some time in the perfect world, you'll automatically start making adaptations to the real world. The perfect-world exercise helps you define your priorities and develop a vision of how you'd like your kitchen to work and look. Once you've considered that vision, you'll need to apply the real-world parameters that act as limits and to start to design a kitchen that works for you. For most of us, those real-world parameters include money, time, and space. In the next three chapters, we're going to consider these parameters and other existing conditions that will affect the process of designing your kitchen.

CHAPTER 2

Money and Budgets

Your kitchen is the most expensive room in the house. Not only is it filled with cabinetry and built-in storage, appliances, seating, utensils, and cookware, but it also is a point where all the hidden mechanical systems of the house converge, including electricity, water, waste disposal, heating and air-conditioning, lighting, even telephone wiring and cable TV.

The kitchen is expensive relative to other rooms because it has many more built-in furnishings and storage spaces and more square feet of surfaces requiring decoration, including counters, backsplashes, ceilings, soffits, flooring, cabinet doors, and drawer fronts. These surfaces are subject to more wear and tear than those found in other rooms. They are attacked by heat, cleaning chemicals, overzealous scrubbing, traffic, and the constant use associated with a room that is often the hub of the house's social activity.

It is also a room filled with cooking tools. Besides the major appliances, literally hundreds of other items are found in every kitchen, including pots and pans, utensils, dishes, linens, small appliances, cleaning supplies, food items like spices and condiments, and furniture. Starting from scratch, equipping even a small kitchen can be alarmingly expensive.

The materials used in kitchens also contribute to the expense. Something as fundamental as a countertop can range in cost from $3 per sq. ft. for laminate to $100 per sq. ft. for stone or ceramic surfaces. When you consider that an average small kitchen has about 30 sq. ft. of counter space, that granite countertop you've been craving suddenly becomes a very expensive consideration. Add in exotic hardwoods for cabinetry, tile floors, wall coverings, and other costly choices, and you have an expensive project.

Remodeling and Return on Investment

There are many theories on whether building a new kitchen is a worthwhile investment in your home's value. Most real estate appraisers claim that a remodeled kitchen returns more of your investment than other remodeled rooms when you sell, but few claim that you'll get all your money back. From our experience, investing in a kitchen must be based on many more factors than return on investment. Your new kitchen should positively change the way you live on a daily basis. In today's fast-moving world, anything that enhances the quality of life and reduces stress has a value that is not measurable by conventional standards.

The value of your kitchen project as an investment is also highly dependent on many factors, including where you live, the existing kitchen you're upgrading or replacing, and the demographics of your neighborhood. If you live in an upscale city neighborhood filled with young professionals, putting in a high-tech, glossy kitchen with stainless-steel restaurant-quality appliances and designer lighting may give your house the "wow" factor you need when you sell. The same kitchen in a suburban tract area filled with young families may not return the cost.

It may help to consider the cost of your kitchen in relation to the overall market value of your house. For our purposes, market value is defined as what an average buyer will pay for your house, not what you believe it is worth. It probably doesn't make sense to put a $50,000 kitchen in a $100,000

house, even if you think you'll be there forever. According to recent estimates, the average American will move seven times in his lifetime, so there's no guarantee that your priorities now will be the same a few years down the road.

Because your kitchen is an expensive room, money becomes an important consideration early in the design process. Whether you're doing a simple remodel or building an elaborate restaurant-style kitchen, you should have a budget in mind from the beginning that you can use to guide the myriad decisions involved in the process. All kitchens have the same basic functions, including:

- efficient use of storage areas
- space for preparation of food
- a cooking surface and oven
- cold storage
- easy access to the rest of the house and an entryway
- a place to clean up and a source of water
- a traffic pattern that is functional

More money simply means better quality, more of everything, more design work, highly crafted detailing, and a general freedom of choice that is limited in a basic kitchen.

In this chapter, we'll provide three models for budgeting based on a basic, mid-level, and high-end kitchen. These models will show you what kinds of choices you have in each range, for everything from architectural design to building materials, and they will help you to make realistic choices. They'll also help you to choose more economical routes and find money for special items you've always wanted.

The use of high-quality materials and well-designed details like the patterned floor in this kitchen are signs of a higher budget. The result is functional and appealing without being ostentatious.

The Basic Kitchen

There are situations where creating a basic kitchen that is functional and attractive without spending a lot of money is the best approach. Even if you have a limited budget, you can, through careful design choices, have a kitchen that works without breaking the bank. The challenge in designing a basic kitchen is to make the most cost-effective use of your space, your money, and the time involved in putting it together. This doesn't mean you have to buy substandard cabinetry or cheap surfacing materials; it may mean you have to work with less storage space, simple finishes, and basic, functional appliances. Fortunately, the range of kitchen cabinetry and materials available for basic kitchens has exploded in recent years. Automated cabinet factories and engineered wood products combined with European design innovation have made it possible to get a quality, well-designed kitchen on a basic budget.

So what is a basic kitchen? A basic kitchen is one that is comfortable and works well yet fits into a limited budget. It is normally a place that is used by only a few people at one time, has less traffic, and has small spaces to work with. Starter homes, apartments, condos designed for working singles or retirees, and vacation homes are all places where it makes sense to limit your budget on a kitchen renovation.

BASIC-KITCHEN DESIGN CHOICES

Creating a budget for a basic kitchen is an exercise in determining how to use resources efficiently. You have to look at what you have and work within the confines of your budget and your existing space. You will be limited in the number of structural or architectural changes you can make, the price of appliances, and the nature of the surfacing materials you use. Often you can forgo an expensive option, but you should still put the necessary connections in during construction so that you can upgrade in the future. For example, if central air-conditioning doesn't fit into your budget now, you should still consider installing the necessary ductwork while the walls are open for a future upgrade. Adding a structurally integrated element like ductwork after a renovation is expensive and difficult. (For design options, see the chart on p. 204.)

Your basic budget must address the following areas. (Those who are planning more expensive kitchens must also address these areas and more, so don't skip this section.)

Design and planning If you don't have a lot of money to pay designers for your whole project, consider at least having the basic layout done by a trained kitchen planner. A designer can anticipate problems, saving money in the long run.

A well-designed kitchen can be built on a restricted budget. Even with limited storage space and simple finishes, this basic kitchen works efficiently and is visually appealing.

Current kitchen space The space you have to work with will either limit or liberate you when budgeting for your kitchen. You save considerable money by sticking with the basic existing architecture and avoiding major demolition and movement of structural elements. However, if your space suffers from typical problems like too many doorways, physical obstructions like chimneys and stairways, and outdated systems, a major tearout may mean savings in the future. (No matter what, don't make structural changes without building permits and qualified contractors who know how to make these changes safely. The structural integrity of your entire house can be compromised by poor construction.)

Existing cabinetry and appliances Reusing some of what you have now can save money. Often, some existing cabinetry, pantries, and other storage bins can be reused and restored with new doors and drawer fronts or with carefully applied new finishes. We've seen many kitchens upgraded successfully with a combination of old and new work topped off by new counter surfacing and paint or refinished wood. Appliances, if in good working order, can be reused.

Floors, walls, and ceilings The surfaces of your new kitchen can eat up a lot of money or very little, depending on the choices you make. Vinyl flooring is cheaper than wood flooring, paint is cheaper than wall covering, and a flat drywall ceiling costs less than a beamed or wood-covered ceiling. These inexpensive surfacing decisions do not mean compromising quality. There are high-quality synthetic floor tiles made for restaurant

use that are extremely durable and attractive and that carry a low price tag. A good paint job costs no more than a poor one; it just means taking your time and/or hiring a skilled pro to do the job. Avoiding complex drywall and plaster work also saves money.

Systems Systems are what we call everything designed to deliver functionality to your kitchen and to remove waste. Because the major components of all systems are buried in the structure of the building, it is vital to plan for and install the finest quality you can afford. This is a place to go overboard even in a basic kitchen. If you overbuild your systems now, like providing more electrical outlets and efficient ductwork, you can improve the quality of your kitchen without straining your budget, provided you deal with these systems now rather than later.

New cabinetry Kitchen cabinets vary in price from inexpensive boxes and doors made of pressed wood to freestanding pieces built like fine furniture and carrying similar price tags. The really low-budget cabinets will not hold up to wear and tear, and their finishes will start looking bad very soon after installation. For a little more money you can get a quality box and door that are solid, well finished, and functional. Add in stylish hardware, and you'll get a great look for a small price (see the photos above right). Even more important, choose your cabinetry based on how you'll use it rather than on quantity, and you'll be able to buy better quality without sacrificing functionality.

Stylish cabinet hardware can help lift a basic kitchen to a mid-level kitchen.

New appliances Lower-priced kitchen appliances are of much higher quality than ever because of breakthroughs in design and technology, laws designed to improve safety, environmental concerns, and bigger markets. Buy good-quality replaceable appliances like stoves and refrigerators and better-quality built-in appliances like sinks and dishwashers.

Today high-quality appliances are made to the same dimensions as their less-expensive counterparts, meaning you can always upgrade from a standard oven to that convection oven without remodeling your kitchen.

Sinks get a lot of wear and tear and are not always as easy to replace, so buying quality now will pay off later.

Lighting Good lighting is often the difference between a great basic kitchen and a poor one. The days of your entire kitchen being lit by one overhead fixture are past, yet we still see new kitchens built with this poor lighting. When you remodel and tear out a kitchen, you have a great opportunity to install a range of general, task, and accent lighting without incurring big fixture bills. Recessed, track, undercabinet, and other lighting is not expensive and can make an incredible difference in the ambience of your new kitchen. Adding this lighting later is expensive because adding wiring for switches and fixtures is difficult after construction is complete. Even if you can't get the expensive designer lighting you want now, wire for it and use inexpensive fixtures in the meantime.

Windows and doors The location of windows and doors can have a major impact on the budget of your new kitchen. Moving existing openings or adding new ones is expensive, yet the increases in usable space, improved traffic flow, and enhanced natural light and airflow can make it worth it. Whatever you do, make the decision to move or add windows and doors before you begin construction. One of the more common cost increases we run into is the result of moving windows and doors after construction has progressed. Changing these architectural elements requires new plans, and that costs money. Don't design by building and rebuilding. Design by visualizing and working on paper before you build.

Traffic flow The way you and your family move through, in, and around your kitchen will affect cost. Simple traffic patterns end up costing less than patterns that work around islands and peninsulas, numerous work spaces, and connected rooms and outdoor areas. A galley kitchen with one entrance may cost less to construct than a larger kitchen due to less cabinetry, less surface area to be decorated, and straight lines rather than complex angles requiring custom fitting and craftsmanship. Islands and peninsulas, while they often add interest and function, also add considerable expense, especially when they include sinks or other appliances requiring utility and waste lines. Numerous entrances also add to costs because they require extra materials and work. For instance, each time you end a run of cabinets next to a door you need to deal with—and pay for—additional exposed surface and finished counter edging.

Keeping traffic patterns simple does not mean sacrificing function or comfort. If you have a logical spot for an island, use a worktable or other movable work surface until you can afford a permanent island. Many European kitchens have functioned well for hundreds of years with freestanding work pieces rather than with built-ins, and you can always add a built-in later without expensive remodeling (if you've planned for it in advance).

Future upgrades Planning to add or upgrade various features is a great way to keep overall costs down without limiting your possibilities. While we all tend to want everything now, there is a definite planning benefit to holding off on certain items like expensive appliances, unusual cabinetry, or complex wall surfacing—you can get a feel for how your basic design is working and make changes as use demands them rather than on impulse. Plan your upgrade path to ensure that all hidden and built-in connections exist for items you're contemplating adding in the future. For instance, if you have your eye on a high-power commercial gas cooktop, make sure you install pressurized gas lines that fit the requirements of your dream appliance, and take care to plan adequate ventilation to handle the heat and smoke generated by big burners. Even if the stove is few years away in your budget, you should install these systems now to save.

The Mid-Level Kitchen

The next step up in both budget and design sophistication is the mid-level kitchen (see the photo on the facing page). Mid-level is not simply a budgetary description. It also describes the degree of function and finish involved. The owners of mid-level kitchens tend to be a little older and more established, both financially and in their habits and use patterns, and they have more resources to work with.

MID-LEVEL DESIGN CHOICES

All of the design considerations for the basic kitchen on pp. 24-26 apply here, but you now have more choices. This is a double-edged sword from a design standpoint. Many of the best designs are the result of working within various constraints, including money, time, and limited space. Often these constraints require creative thinking to come up with the solutions that define good design. Having a little more money and a little more flexibility can mean having a lot more choices, and having those choices can result in the kid-in-the-candy-store syndrome: a form of mental gridlock caused by having so many choices that you cannot make any for fear of making the wrong ones.

When you're working on a basic budget you have a model for decision making: Is this the best choice for the money in the context of the design? The creators of a mid-level kitchen can also use this model, but they must add to it. This is where professional design help and a good overall plan become vital to creating a successful kitchen. If you are looking for one cost-effective place to spend more time and money, it is on planning.

A more expensive kitchen is not necessarily a larger kitchen. Nor is it a more functional kitchen. And it is unlikely to have significantly differing functions than a basic kitchen. You still cook, clean up, socialize, and store there. The differences may be in the types and the technology of your appliances, surfaces, and lighting and in the types of systems like water, cleanup, and waste removal. You may have more cabinets, more built-ins, more use of natural surfacing materials, architectural detailing, and the option of moving or adding windows and entrances.

You may also be able to make structural changes to the room, adding windows and walls or relocating entrances. These structural changes may be made to facilitate utility upgrades, enhance lighting, and relocate appliances. Large-scale structural changes

A mid-level budget allows for custom cabinetry with a higher level of architectural detail.

like additions may raise the overall budget into the high-end range. Plan carefully before committing to major construction. (For design options, see the chart on p. 204.)

Appliances Your appliances will be more durable, have more sophisticated functions, and present a higher level of aesthetic design involving finishes like stainless steel and high-tech ceramics. You are likely to have more appliances than the standard ones. Your portable appliance selection is likely to be larger and require more space and sufficient power supply. Adding an item like a professional-quality mixer means more than simply purchasing the mixer; it means having a dedicated place for this heavy, high-wattage machine where you can get the best use out of it. This in turn may mean additional counter space, an appliance garage, or a pop-up, undercabinet mixer stand. All must be planned and budgeted for.

Surfaces You have many more choices in surface materials in the mid-level kitchen than in the basic kitchen. This includes more choices in solid materials as opposed to surfaces applied to a substrate, like laminate over fiberboard. Solid-core, man-made counter materials, for example, simulate the appearance and function of stone. While these solid materials are very durable and attractive, they also are more difficult to install and often require specialized skills and tools, making their overall price higher.

At the mid-level, you'll probably be mixing custom-fabricated items with good-quality factory-built pieces. Cabinetry, counters, and furniture items all present you with this choice of custom versus manufactured. Try to remain open-minded. In many cases, you will have a very large range of options with a manufactured product, sometimes more than can be provided by a custom fabricator. For instance, factory-applied finishes are usually very durable and uniform because specialized machinery and operators do nothing else but apply them.

Good designers faced with budget limitations often choose a few high-quality parts and integrate them with

In high-end kitchens, you have the opportunity to make significant architectural changes. The owners of this kitchen chose a grand look by adding pillars and an arched ceiling above the sink. (Photo by Louis Mackall.)

good-quality pieces to convey an overall sense of detail and craftsmanship. Simple items like cabinet pulls can change the appearance of a whole kitchen in an almost indefinable way (see the photos on p. 25). Pulls range in price from a few dollars each for simple mass-produced types to very expensive handmade versions. Making stylish and functional choices on these ubiquitous and tactile items can lift an ordinary cabinet up to the next level.

Lighting When asked what design decision makes the biggest difference for the money, we have chosen lighting. Time after time, new kitchen owners are amazed at the difference functional, clearly lit work surfaces and a choice of light levels and placement can make. Few standard kitchens installed by home-builders and few remodel jobs place any emphasis on good lighting design, yet even a small number of fixtures designed for specific uses and carefully located can make an incredible difference in the overall ambience and comfort of your kitchen. In a mid-level kitchen you can usually afford a full range of lighting. (Lighting will be covered in detail in Chapter 6.)

Water, cleanup, and waste removal

After designing and working in dozens of kitchens, it's our experience that, unlike the kitchens of the past that centered around the hearth, the modern kitchen works around the sink and cleanup areas, so you'll want to carefully consider what you buy and where you'll use it. A high-quality sink is worth buying because it is more durable, insulated to reduce noise, and designed ergonomically to be easy to work in without splashing water all over the place. The range of choices in color, shape, and size is wide.

If you're considering adding an additional sink for food preparation or a bar area, be aware that it requires a lot of hidden plumbing, including water supply lines, drains, and drain venting. You may need a dedicated electrical circuit and switch if you install a disposal in the extra sink. Installing the plumbing requires a plumber and should be done before any walls are closed up. If you decide to put a sink in an island, you'll want to consult a plumber to make sure it is physically possible to locate the proper lines without doing major reconstruction. We'll cover the challenges involved with these systems in more detail in Chapter 4.

High-end kitchens are often dream kitchens. When your budget is high, you can splurge on commercial appliances like a Sub-Zero refrigerator, a natural tile floor, and extensive lighting to create the kitchen you desire. (Photo by Wayne Simco.)

The High-End Kitchen

The kitchen has the potential to be the most expensive room in the house, and it most certainly will be when you venture into the incredible range of choices available when the sky's the limit (or at least a piece of the sky). While there are many very expensive kitchens in which virtually every as-

pect is custom designed and fabricated, this discussion is limited to kitchens having an "average" high budget of $30,000 to $40,000. This high budget gets you excellent design talent, impeccable craftsmanship, the best materials, and world-class appliances. Or, at least it should. Unfortunately it is quite possible to throw enormous resources into a kitchen and still end up with a bad design that is poorly executed.

Good design techniques at work in higher-budget kitchens include a balanced use of quality materials like these granite counters and the tile wall and the integration of appliances like this European cooktop and oven.

$50,000 to $60,000 or more on a kitchen without using a designer. The more knowledge you have about kitchen design, the better you will be able to communicate your needs and desires to your designer and the more likely you are to get a great kitchen in exchange for your money.

Expensive kitchens have an element of fantasy about them. Re-creating a restaurant kitchen in your home may really be about living out an unrealized dream of being a chef. Or it may fulfill a very real need for a workplace for you to seriously pursue an interest in cooking. Either way (and it's likely to be both), that kitchen is still about the same things as the basic and mid-level kitchens we discussed earlier: comfort, socializing, preparing and serving food, and cleaning up. The big difference is that every decision involves a lot more money.

High-end kitchens often involve significant architectural changes to the building, expensive surfacing materials like stone, tile, and exotic hardwoods, and commercial appliances. Much of the added cost comes from the attention to detail and craftsmanship required by custom kitchen design. Quality consumes time, and in the construction world time is expensive. (For design options, see the chart on p. 204.)

It is tempting to dwell on the potential for disaster at this level because too often high end means a lot of money was spent rather than a lot of creative effort. Anyone with deep pockets can fill a room with a zillion cabinets, $20,000 to $30,000 worth of major appliances, imported tile, 18-color hand-screened French wallpaper, hand-polished silver-plated sinks, and Neo-Georgian moldings. Whether this conglomeration of excess actually works is up to the designer, and if you're spending this kind of money for a kitchen, you should seek out a good one. In Chapter 5, we'll discuss how to go about finding and working with a designer.

While talking about money and the upper end of the kitchen world, it is best to focus on how a designer can help you get what you want while spending enough but not too much. It is rare for a homeowner to spend

Budgets and Perfection

One of the challenges in designing and budgeting for any great kitchen is achieving perfection. In our experience, perfection is seldom found in this world, with the possible exceptions of great art, Zen gardens, and Olympic athletes. Yet we persist in this futile search for a kitchen that fulfills our dreams of a perfect space. And, during the initial creative part of kitchen design, there's nothing wrong with setting high goals. The problem occurs when we try to combine that search with the real world of existing house, a stubborn contractor, undelivered necessities, and a dwindling checking account.

The solution lies in putting together a working timeline and budget for your project before you tear out a wall or shop for appliances. Time and money are inexorably intertwined, especially when you are facing a construction delay in the middle of a long kitchenless period of your life because a range hood you had to have is back-ordered. It is important to start thinking about money and time now, while you're reading this book and gathering ideas. In Part 3, we'll look at construction planning and how your budget may change at that stage, but here are some suggestions to consider now:

- Give yourself back-up choices on everything if possible. Availability of almost any component of a kitchen can suddenly disappear, throwing well-laid plans awry.
- Research price ranges for various items when starting a budget, picking a price level that works in your situation. If you budget $1,000 for a range rather than choosing a specific brand, you'll be thinking in terms of content, which can be substituted if things change.
- Walk through your space with an architect or a skilled carpenter, and make plans showing structural walls and the location of utility lines, drains, etc. This information will help you budget for major moves of these potentially expensive structures.
- Catalog existing features that stay, like windows, moldings, flooring, appliances, built-in cabinetry, etc.

Every dollar you spend will be affected by the planning and choices you make. Projects go over budget because of last-minute changes, inflexibility, indecision, underestimates that are often the result of going with the lowest bid on an item, poor scheduling, and unsuspected obstacles uncovered as you go. Good planning can help prevent all of these.

Financing Your Kitchen

While this is not a book about personal finance, let's look at a few relevant areas regarding where to get the money for your project. Kitchens are improvements to what is usually the biggest investment most of us will ever make, our homes. Because the improvements are fixed, with a long life, taking out a mortgage or home-equity loan to fund them may make sense. However, there is no guarantee that they will increase the market value of your home, and if you are planning a move in the near future, you should be careful about how much you spend, especially if you don't have a lot of equity in your home.

It takes cash to build a kitchen. Contractors must be paid upon completion, appliance stores expect payment or credit with interest, and you'll seem to be spending everywhere you go for zillions of little things you didn't expect. Keep track of every expenditure and check it against your budget. If you have a computer with a spreadsheet program, you may want to use it to track your costs and keep an ongoing tally that lets you know if you're going over budget. Otherwise, it will be worthwhile to keep track on paper, not forgetting all those little cash expenses during those innumerable trips to the hardware store.

If you realize in your tracking that you're going over budget and you don't have a cheaper alternative to fall back on, ask for advice. Designers, suppliers, and contractors know a lot of ways to save money on almost any aspect of the job. Sometimes a simple design change can save significant money. Compromise is required, but it's better than ignoring the problem or going into debt for something cosmetic.

Designing and building anything as complex as a kitchen is an incredible learning experience. Even before the actual process, you'll find out many things you wouldn't have dreamed of. Some of these will be good, and others will involve stress and a degree of fear, including making difficult decisions, handling contractors, and coping with mistakes. Many of these potentially negative experiences revolve around money and how it flows through the project. Plan now, do your research, and make a budget and schedule, and you'll avoid a lot these problems.

CHAPTER 3
The Kitchen in Motion

Your kitchen is unique among the rooms in your home in that it is a hub of activity for everyone in the household. It usually has more than one entrance, connects to other rooms and the outdoors, and has areas designed for specific functions that are interrelated. You may rinse a pan at the sink, fill it with water and move it to a stove, add food prepped at another spot, cook at the stove, and head back to the sink to drain off the hot water. The pan eventually gets washed and stored, often above your head or below your knees, requiring motion in those directions. All the while you may be conversing, coaching children doing their homework nearby, or watching the evening news on a convenient TV.

These ranges of motion make designing a kitchen that works well a challenge. In this chapter, we're going to look at how you move in your kitchen and how you can start thinking in three dimensions and in terms of movement in, through, and around your kitchen. And how, by following ergonomic guidelines, you can make those movements more comfortable and safe. But movement is not limited to people; it also includes light, airflow, and the range of motion of cabinet, appliance, and entry doors. Understanding potential conflicts and their solutions is important to a well-planned kitchen. This is the start of the actual design process, and if you plan well now, you'll end up with a far more functional kitchen.

Three-Dimensional Thinking

One of the hardest concepts to grasp about interior design is that it is not a two-dimensional process. We're so used to seeing builders pouring over blueprints and floor plans that it is easy to start thinking exclusively in terms of two-dimensional patterns. Architects, designers, and builders may look at these flat drawings, but they think of them in terms of a three-dimensional space. The two-dimensional language of drafting and construction drawings made this visualization necessary. Now with the advent of three-dimensional CAD (computer-aided design) software for personal computers, it is possible to view your environment in three di-

mensions, to freely apply and move various elements around, and even to "walk" through the project, all before any actual construction takes place.

This technology can help teach inexperienced people to think visually and to consider their kitchen as a room with three dimensions rather than as a floor plan or elevation. (An elevation is a two-dimensional drawing that shows a slice of a room from top to bottom, such as a wall of cabinetry viewed head-on. See the top illustration on the facing page.) While three-dimensional CAD software is widely available, it often has a steep learning curve and requires a lot of computing power. Even with sophisticated CAD programs, a basic understanding of how the planning process works is a necessity.

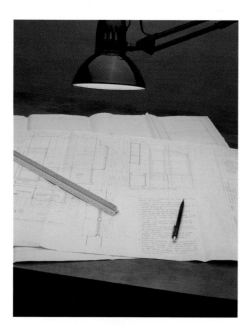

One of the biggest design challenges you'll face is translating two-dimensional plans like these into a three-dimensional kitchen space.

Plan Drawing

A two-dimensional plan shows the view from directly overhead.

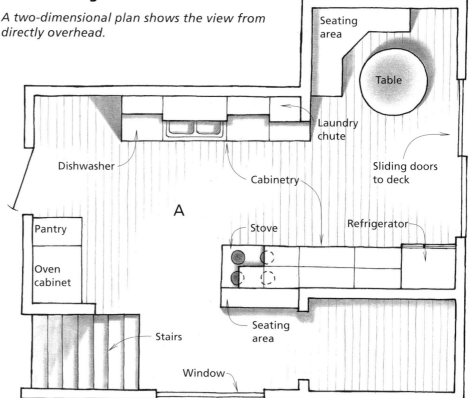

The first step is understanding how your current kitchen works and how it can be improved. We're going to walk you through a process for evaluating the motion in your existing kitchen. It starts with making sketches of what's in your kitchen (see the illustration on the facing page). Once you've decided how your kitchen needs to work, you can begin the process of physically designing your space. Even if you work with a designer, this exercise will give you insight into how the design process can enhance the final usefulness of the kitchen space.

Traffic Flow

The primary motion in a kitchen is traffic flow. Unless you live alone, you'll be sharing this room with others while doing complex and potentially dangerous tasks. Even if you do live by

"Elevation A" from the Plan Drawing

This elevation drawing is what you would see if you were standing at A on the illustration on the facing page.

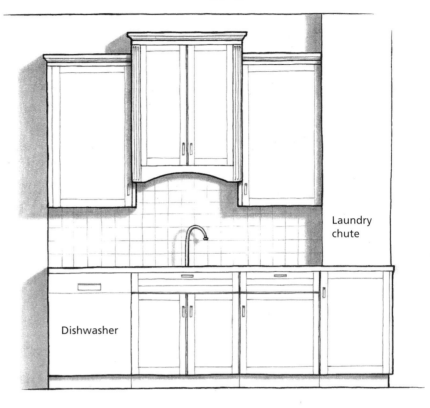

Laundry chute

Dishwasher

Everyday Kitchen Traffic

This drawing illustrates both everyday traffic through and around the kitchen and the cook's motion within the work area of the kitchen.

Solid lines: everyday traffic through the kitchen to the outside

Dotted lines: the cook's movements

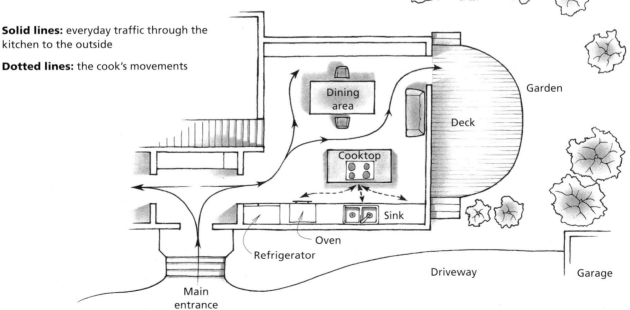

Dining area

Garden

Deck

Cooktop

Sink

Oven

Refrigerator

Main entrance

Driveway

Garage

yourself, you will be working and living in the room on several levels, from enjoying a quiet cup of coffee at a seating area to carrying in bags of groceries at the end of a busy day. If your kitchen has limited space to leave a coffee cup or set down a heavy bag, you'll soon be stuck in your own personal traffic jam.

Traffic flow in a kitchen comes in four varieties: movement through and around the work areas of the kitchen, movement in task-specific areas, movement between the kitchen and other areas of the house, and movement between the kitchen and the outside. Ideally these four ranges of motion do not conflict, but realistically they will. When you start planning the layout of your new kitchen, start with

an overall floor-plan sketch of your kitchen and surrounding areas as they exist now, before remodeling, and include outdoor areas (see the bottom illustration on p. 35). Don't worry about cabinets or appliances. Instead, look at the way traffic flows in and out of the kitchen on a daily basis. Draw in lines for the most heavily traveled routes into and through the kitchen to show you spaces and pathways that should not be obstructed. Think of this flow as water seeking the path of least resistance.

WORK TRIANGLE

The traditional model for traffic flow in a kitchen is the classic work triangle describing the relationship between

the stove, sink, and refrigerator as seen from overhead. The work triangle is a viable way of evaluating a design at the basic level because it keeps you from making one of these areas inaccessible to the others or from creating long walks with hot pans, a sink that's too far from food-prep areas, etc. However, we've found that it works better to consider the sink as the primary staging area for preparation and cleanup.

Sink areas tend to be used at the start, middle, and end of the cooking process. For this reason, your work triangle or traffic pattern should focus on the relationship between the sink area and the counter or work spaces in between it and other appliances. Place your sink so you can easily access it

The Work Triangle

The sink is a central work area in the kitchen. Your work triangle should focus on the relationship between the sink, the range, and the refrigerator and their connecting work spaces.

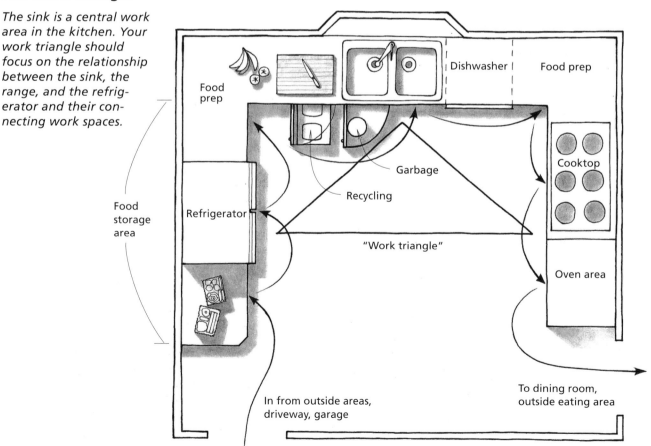

Food prep

Dishwasher

Food prep

Food prep

Garbage

Recycling

Cooktop

Food storage area

Refrigerator

"Work triangle"

Oven area

In from outside areas, driveway, garage

To dining room, outside eating area

from the refrigerator and the stove, preferably with dedicated work spaces in between. Imagine you are removing vegetables from the refrigerator for a recipe. They go to the sink for rinsing and then to a cutting board for preparation. Then they go into a pan for cooking, then into an oven for more cooking or warming or directly into a serving dish. That dish in turn goes to the table and then back to the sink area to complete the cycle. It turns out that the spaces in between the appliances of the work triangle are just as important as the appliance placement itself (see the illustration on the facing page).

ISOLATION AREAS

In addition to continuous movement through and around the kitchen, there is movement into specific areas for specific reasons. A common example is coming in from the car with groceries. You walk in with your arms full and immediately seek a place to set things down. That spot should be near the door without obstructing the ongoing traffic flow you sketched in earlier. These "dead-end," or staging, spots are isolation areas that are reserved for specific activities—counter space reserved for incoming bags or a writing area with a phone for taking messages, checking recipes, or paying bills (see the top photo at right). You'll probably want to keep a clear path from where you store your garbage to the outside area where it is deposited. This path should be clear of obstructions like open cabinet doors, chairs, and tables.

Left: *This small peninsula provides an isolation area for meal planning and cookbook storage.*

Below: *Separation doesn't have to mean isolation. The cook working behind this island cooktop is still in touch with the social area of the room.*

Right: *Easy access to a rear deck from the driveway encourages guests to go directly to the outdoor entertainment area outside the kitchen. Photo taken at A on the illustration on the facing page.*

Below: *This view from the garden shows the curved deck and a row of glass doors connecting it to the kitchen. Photo taken at B on the illustration on the facing page.*

These task-specific isolation areas can come in other forms. An avid cook who entertains frequently and enjoys socializing while cooking may create a barrier of cabinetry like an island or peninsula to maintain separation between the cooking space and her guests (see the bottom photo on p. 37). The same layout may serve to keep children out of a potentially dangerous situation during food preparation without banning them from the room.

THE REST OF THE LIVING SPACE

Flow between rooms is also important. Doorways to dining areas must be wide enough to carry hot dishes back and forth comfortably, the connection to a family room may need to be close if you eat casual meals or take-out food in there, and a clear path into the kitchen from the main entry that by-passes the more formal living areas may be desirable.

In all of these cases, the motion should be as unobstructed as possible and should end in the kitchen at a specific destination. Dishes from the dining room will be headed toward the sink or dishwasher, but you'll want a place to pile them up as you clear a table quickly. You may also want easy access to trash receptacles and recycling bins.

THE OUTDOORS

Today interaction between the kitchen and outdoor living areas is very important. You will obviously want clear pathways between parking areas and the kitchen storage areas. But if you spend a lot of time outdoors cooking, entertaining, gardening, and relaxing, you'll probably want access to deck or

A wall of glass doors visually brings the outdoor entertainment areas and garden into the kitchen. Photo taken at C on the illustration below.

Integration of the Outside and Interior Living Areas

Traffic flow between the driveway, garden, deck, and kitchen is carefully planned for entertaining and for easy access to the kitchen.

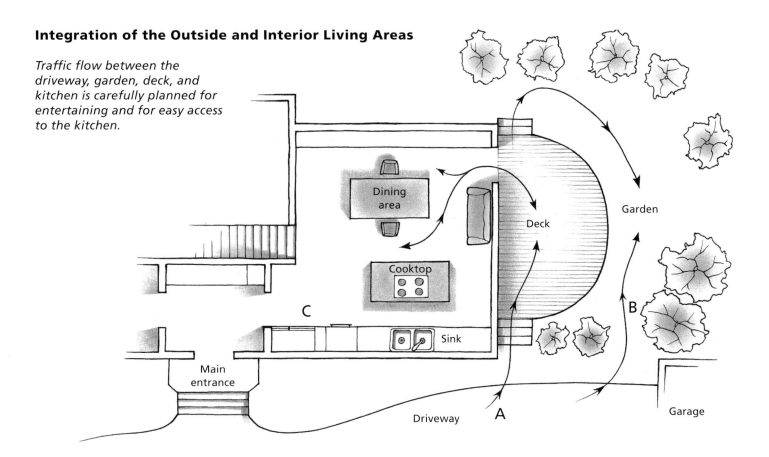

Dining area

Cooktop

C

Sink

Main entrance

Garden

Deck

B

Driveway

A

Garage

patio areas, too. Gardeners will want easy access into the kitchen, too, for preparing their homegrown vegetables and for arranging their flowers.

Light and Airflow

Bringing the outdoors in also means thinking in terms of light and airflow. Windows, French doors, and skylights all contribute copious quantities of natural light and a fresh flow of air. If your present kitchen is dark, lacks windows, or has small or obstructed views, adding even one carefully placed window or skylight can make an enormous difference in the overall feel of the space.

The views outside your kitchen windows and doors can extend the depth of a small room, provide a source of vibrant color, and add the illusion of additional space. But they can also have a negative effect, reminding you that you're in a busy city neighborhood or a little too close to a highway. Clever use of window treatments, outdoor plantings and fences, and soundproof building materials can turn away that noisy din and turn your kitchen into an oasis of silence and softened light. Windows act as frames for outdoor scenes and can be placed to highlight part of a view or to hide an unsightly one (see the photo at right).

But light is not the only element that flows in your kitchen space. Air flows, too, carrying heat, cold, and odors and fragrances in, around, and through the room. We call an airless room stuffy; yet even a small room with a good source of clean, fresh air will feel expansive and open. Cooking, trash, and building materials all create gases that are smelly and potentially

Here, a small window over a countertop acts as a source of light and a frame for the constantly changing garden view. The designer could have filled the spot with cabinetry but instead used it to add depth to the interior.

noxious. Modern building materials often contain chemicals that are released over time, resulting in that overpowering smell you encounter in building-supply stores. For several months after construction, you'll experience outgassing as your carpets, wood finishes, plastic laminates, and other materials complete their long-term curing process.

Designing for adequate airflow is the next step on your floor-plan sketch. Heat and air-conditioning ducts and returns must be located, ventilation ductwork for ranges and ovens must be connected to an outside vent, and waste lines for water systems must be located. Water drains do not only go down in buildings; they must also have pipes leading up and outside to eliminate suction and to release sewage gases out of the house. Unless you're an experienced plumber, you may not be aware of this network of large pipes built into your walls and protruding from your roof line. In the next chapters, we'll look at identifying and designing around these hidden systems.

With air pollution a fact of life in many areas, airflow may also include filtration systems to remove pollutants, cigarette smoke, and animal dander. Allergy sufferers may need filtration to remove pollen and dust particles. Air-filtration systems often share ductwork with heat and air-conditioning.

Like the flow of natural light, air enters your space through doors and windows. But doors and windows create obstacles that must be placed on your sketch and worked around when considering your traffic flow. The direction your doors open is a critical traffic-flow decision. Light switches need to be located on the opening side of a door, and the path of the door should not obstruct traffic flow when it's open. If a door opens into a room, it requires space to open fully. Windows need to be accessible if you open them regularly, and skylights may require powered openers operated by wall switches.

Islands in the Stream

Diagramming the motion of people, light, and air through your empty space will result in areas that naturally remain clear of traffic on your floor-plan sketch. If these areas fall in the middle of a room, they may be potential locations for tables or fixed islands of cabinetry. When these open spaces are located near a wall, a peninsula or bar area may fit in. If you cannot locate a natural spot for groceries, socializing, or other activities along a wall, adding an island may be the solution.

Placing an island or table in a kitchen should not be automatic. An island requires considerable space around it to function well and, if it is to contain a sink, range, or other appliance, utility connections can be a challenge. All too often we've found a homeowner has been unwittingly talked into an island by a cabinet salesperson who recognizes an opportunity to double the cabinet order on an otherwise small kitchen. A small island measuring 3 ft. by 6 ft. (18 sq. ft.) requires as much as 125 sq. ft. of floor space when you add in a 3-ft.-wide access corridor around it, which is the reasonable minimum required for two people to work in an area (see the illustration below).

Optimum Work Corridors

Even a small island requires considerable floor area to work well.

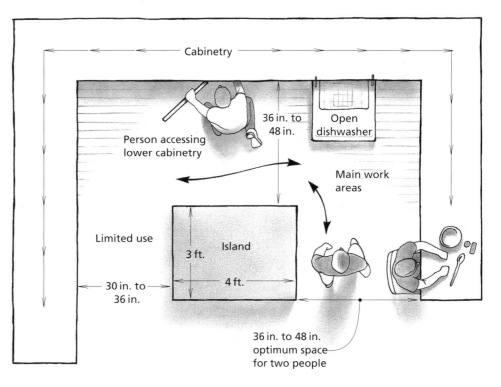

Hidden Ductwork

Cabinetry can serve as a place to run ductwork and wiring. This duct is built into the kick area of the lower cabinets.

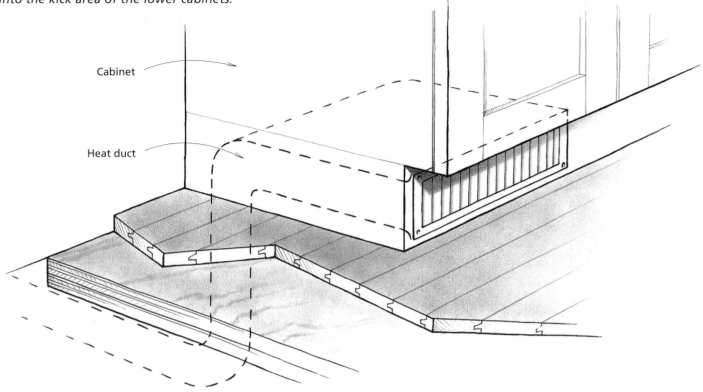

Cabinet

Heat duct

Fixed Elements

Besides the areas you defined as isolation areas for specific tasks, such as desks and counters, there are a number of fixed items in every kitchen, and these must be identified on the floor-plan sketch. These include cabinetry, major appliances permanently connected to household systems, and sinks. Certain small appliances like computers and countertop mixers may be immobile because of their weight or size, and they will require dedicated areas. You will also need a large amount of surface area dedicated to food preparation, casual eating, socializing over drinks, speaking on the phone, homework, crafts, and other functions that find their way into your kitchen.

These fixed areas should not block the traffic flow. For this reason, it is common to run blocks of cabinetry along walls, resulting in the typical modern kitchen look of runs of cabinetry surrounding the perimeter of the room. In effect, perimeter cabinets shrink the interior space of the room and replace it with work surfaces over and under storage areas. These cabinets also serve to hide ducts, pipes, and other systems, making it possible to run utility lines into areas of the room that would not be possible in an open space (see the illustration above).

Three-Dimensional Traffic Patterns

To this point, we've focused on two-dimensional traffic patterns of motion. These are basically movements across a room or side to side. Now it's time to consider other ranges of motion, such as up and down and opening and closing. Storage in kitchens is typically above shoulder level or below waist level, meaning you must reach up or bend over. You must also open and close those same storage places. Both of these kinds of motion require space and need to be identified on your floor-plan sketch.

UP AND DOWN

The range of motion up and down means placing items like pot racks and wall-mounted cabinets at a height that is reachable by an average person. If you have a unusually short person regularly using the kitchen, you'll want to consider how that person will function in the space. This may mean storing frequently used items in lower cabinets and reserving out-of-reach space for longer-term storage. We can't recommend building to a height other than what is standard—36 in. for work surfaces—unless you plan to own the property for a long time. An unusually high or low work surface could be a major liability when selling a house.

OPEN AND CLOSE

There is another range of movement in kitchens that if not carefully considered can result in many problems during daily use. This is the motion of doors as they swing through their radius while opening and closing and of drawers as they are pulled out. This is not limited to cabinetry; refrigerators, dishwashers, and ovens also have doors that require considerable space to open fully.

It is tempting to consider the width of a door plus a few inches enough space to leave open in front of a cabinet. However, you may want to pass by an open door, or you may want to open two opposing doors or drawers at the same time, effectively doubling the clearance space required. This is common around dishwashers, the door of which remains open during loading while the user is moving in and out of the room bringing in dishes from another area. Without careful

A difficult floor plan that required locating this refrigerator here meant limiting the freezer door's opening radius.

In this corner, there is a conflict between the top drawer and the dishwasher door due to poor planning.

This isolated corner of a kitchen provides the perfect place for a wood-burning stove, out of the main traffic flow.

To fix the problem, a portion of the protruding drawer front was removed and permanently attached to the cabinet. The drawer opens easily now and appears normal when closed.

planning, you'll find yourself opening and shutting doors to maneuver around others.

On your floor-plan sketch, add in the radius of operation, or range of movement, for all doors and drawers. Sometimes you can use bifold or accordion-style doors or sliding doors to work a cabinet into a tight space, but in general you want to avoid this and design a kitchen that is comfortable to work in. Specialized doors also have their share of challenges, as they usually require extra space, limiting the interior size of the cabinets they are part of.

"Dead" Spaces

Often, after you've spent some time fine-tuning your floor-plan sketch, you'll find you've created inaccessible "dead" spaces. This is common in corners where access via doors only gets you into a fraction of the volume filled by the cabinetry. Sometimes this can be resolved by using revolving interior shelves or pull-out racks that give you full access to interiors. These racks are useful in nearly all lower cabinets because they allow you to use space that typically is not practical to reach into without contorting yourself. Pullouts also work well for very narrow cabinets suited to storing flat items like trays or pot lids. However, they do re-

Above: *This appliance garage uses "dead" space created in a corner to provide storage for small appliances.*

Right: *With the tambour door of the appliance garage pulled down, the counter appears clean and uncluttered.*

Ergonomic Guidelines

The range of human motion is the final criteria for designing the relationship between various elements of your kitchen. For a kitchen to work well it must be comfortably accessible to the average person.

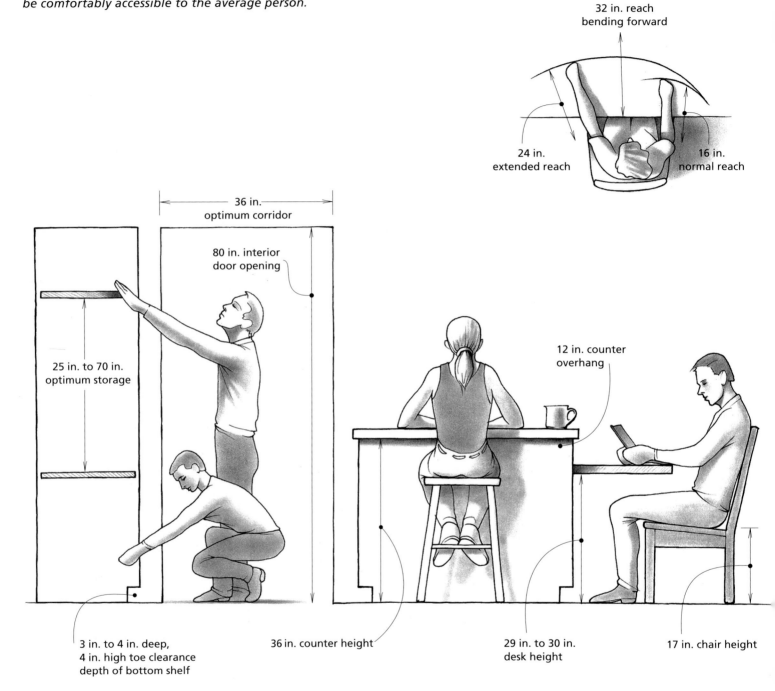

32 in. reach
bending forward

24 in.
extended reach

16 in.
normal reach

36 in.
optimum corridor

80 in. interior
door opening

25 in. to 70 in.
optimum storage

12 in. counter
overhang

3 in. to 4 in. deep,
4 in. high toe clearance
depth of bottom shelf

36 in. counter height

29 in. to 30 in.
desk height

17 in. chair height

quire adequate space in front of the cabinet so they can be fully extended.

Other dead space may not be as obvious. Areas left open behind doors or stretches of wall that are in corridors too narrow for normal cabinetry constitute space that can be used with creative planning. A shallow set of shelves, a flush wall-hung pot rack, or a shallow display cabinet running from floor to ceiling can help utilize these overlooked spaces. These areas are also suitable as cookbook shelves or a narrow pantry. Or you can place a narrow counter in a passageway to use as a buffet or bar area with dish and glass storage below or overhead.

Inaccessible spaces are also good places to put system elements, such as pipes and ducts, appliance garages, and recessed fixtures that can be hidden away and accessed mechanically, such as a pop-up undercabinet mixer stand. For many systems elements you will still need to provide emergency access via a removable panel.

Ergonomics

As you consider what you want your kitchen space to accomplish and how you'd visualize it as a day-to-day work space, you'll start running into questions about what works and what doesn't. How wide an aisle do I need between an island and a counter? How high should the highest shelves be? When is a sink too deep or too shallow? These questions come up constantly while designing anything for human use. Fortunately, the science of ergonomics, which studies the range of human movement and our physical interaction with the world, has defined many of these measure-

ments. Based on the average range of movement of a typical human, ergonomics offers the kitchen designer a set of guidelines for setting heights, widths, and other measurements to ensure safety and comfort in your kitchen (see the illustration on the facing page).

It is important to stick with these guidelines so that your kitchen will work for many users. Even more important, all manufactured kitchen cabinetry, appliances, and accessories use these guidelines to create standard sizes. This means that the recycling-center insert you purchase from one source will fit into a standard cabinet from another source. It also means that carpenters, electricians, and other craftspeople will, unless told otherwise, place cabinets, fixtures, and outlets at standard heights and locations.

Sticking to ergonomic guidelines will save you money in a number of ways. Nonstandard items must be custom crafted at considerably higher cost. Work surfaces located at awkward heights can lead to back problems and repetitive-motion injuries. As noted earlier, odd-sized or nonstandard work spaces can reduce the value of your house.

More than any other consideration, ergonomically correct design will result in a kitchen that is much more convenient and comfortable to use. When you work or socialize with others in the various spaces, you won't get in each other's way while performing different tasks, and you'll be able to spend long periods cooking and cleaning up with less physical stress and strain.

Floor-Plan Development

Your floor-plan sketch is undoubtedly getting pretty complex with a mishmash of traffic lines, areas for cabinetry and other functions, doorways and windows, outlines of existing utility lines, and areas for passage in and out of the space. You have also undoubtedly run into numerous conflicts with windows where counters want to be, doors right where you'd really like to put a range, and immovable objects like staircases and chimneys.

Resolving these conflicts is an exercise in creative thinking and, especially when starting out, requires a lot of trial and error. Experience helps a lot, and this is one area where an experienced designer can iron out a lot of problems. Often the designer can see a solution that you're not aware of that resolves and integrates many of your concerns.

For now, we suggest you play with your floor-plan sketch, keeping it very simple and trying various layouts. (We'll make more detailed plans in Chapter 5.) Don't get bogged down in details about appearances, styles, brands, and other considerations that can come later. Stick to the issues covered in this and the next chapter—traffic flow and existing systems that must be considered early in the process. You'll have plenty of time to decide on a cabinetry style later. Planning the layout has to happen before construction is even considered.

CHAPTER 4

The Hidden Kitchen

You are finally ready to start construction on your new kitchen. The first worker comes in and begins to demolish a wall to enlarge the space you've planned for your dream kitchen. Down comes plaster and lath, and when the dust settles you have a problem. There in the middle of your now-skeletal wall is a 6-in. black iron pipe running from the floor to the ceiling and up. A few feet away is a run of heating duct going from the basement to your master bedroom upstairs. Horizontally the studs are pierced by three rows of electrical wires, going to who knows what. Finally, the worker looks up and observes that the wall looks like a bearing wall, holding up the floor joists of the rooms above. He can't just take it out without installing a large header, or beam, across the opening, ruining your imagined expanse of smooth ceiling.

All of these things exist in the walls of every kitchen, hidden but absolutely necessary to the safe and efficient functioning of your house. Planning a kitchen without identifying these hidden systems is asking for an expensive and messy lesson in home mechanics like our horror tale above.

In the last chapter, when we started working on the way your new kitchen will function, we mentioned these hidden systems as obstructions that must be considered now, before any actual purchasing, budgeting, or construction is done. Only at the design stage can you rearrange and plan around these systems without needlessly spending money and time. Even though most building codes require li-

censed contractors to work on these systems, you'll benefit from a basic knowledge of them.

In this chapter, we're going to look at each hidden system and your options, from a planning point of view, for coping with them. These systems, hidden away under your walls, ceilings, and floors, include electricity and lighting, water supply and waste removal, gas for cooking and heating, air supplies for ventilation and heating, and various wiring for phones, stereos, and security systems. The structural framing of the house itself is also a system designed to bear the weight of the house and to protect it from the elements. All of these systems must conform to legal standards, or codes, for safety and proper operation. Understanding where they are and how they work is essential to planning any changes for your new kitchen.

Codes and Regulations

All of these mechanical structures and systems are regulated by law because of numerous safety and community quality issues. Most community regulations are based on national building codes that specify, in exhaustive detail, how each and every situation must be handled. Following code and using licensed contractors is not only good for your project, but it may also be a legal requirement. Permits must be obtained, a process we'll look at in Part 3. If you skip these requirements and build illegally, many municipalities have the legal right to require you to tear out the offending work and rebuild. As you'll see in this chapter, there are very good reasons for the severity of these laws and codes.

Structural Integrity

All buildings, including houses, are engineered structures designed to handle stress loads and great weights. The foundation, the wall, floor, and roof framing, and the sheathing all work together to provide a structurally sound and weatherproof skeleton and envelope for your home. Properly designed and constructed homes are very solid and offer the secure knowledge that they will last a long time and be safe to inhabit,

Because most homes today are wood-frame structures where stud walls support floor joists that act as platforms for upper floors and roofs, you cannot freely assume that any wall is removable during a reconstruc-

What is it? It's not unusual to encounter old systems buried in your walls during a demolition. Be sure they no longer function before removing them.

tion process. You may wish to double the size of your kitchen by taking over an adjacent space or by building out from an existing one. In both cases, you'll be removing a wall or walls and potentially compromising the entire structural integrity and safety of your home. Some walls, known as non-bearing or curtain walls, serve mainly as room dividers and do not carry a significant structural load. Others, known as bearing walls, carry much of the weight of everything above them.

INTERIOR BEARING WALLS

Moving or removing a bearing wall can be expensive and requires the construction of another structure to replace that wall's load-bearing capacity. This replacement must be done by qualified carpenters and contractors who understand how to figure loads and spans and can design solutions that allow you to remove a wall.

Bearing walls typically run perpendicular to or across the floor joists of the upper floor, supporting these joists; the walls are often near the center of the house. Determining the direction that joists run is the first step in determining whether a wall can be easily moved. Walls running parallel to floor joists are generally nonbearing walls. The problem is that in certain situations it is not always possible to determine if a wall is a bearing wall by looking at visible floor joists in the basement. So, before you plan on moving a wall, ask a contractor or architectural engineer to determine its structural function.

If you discover a wall you want to remove is a bearing wall, it does not mean that it's immovable. You have

A large horizontal beam (referred to as a header) calculated to carry the required load can be substituted when removing a load-bearing wall.

several options. You can replace it with another wall nearby, calculated to safely take over from the old wall. You can also have a header installed, which is a beam spanning the opening created by the removal of the bearing wall (see the photo above). This header is carefully designed, based on mathematical formulas and engineering standards, to hold the weight of the upper building. Its size and what it is made of will be determined by these formulas and by the aesthetic requirements of the design. A wood header may be large and project down into the opening like a cross beam on a beamed ceiling. A metal I-beam or a high-tech, laminated wood I-beam is less intrusive. Long spans may require the rigidity and strength of a metal or laminated wood beam.

As you can imagine, this construction work entails extra time and expense. Removing walls is something that must be planned for early, and you should be aware of the costs and design compromises that may be involved.

OUTSIDE WALLS

You can consider all outside walls as bearing walls that must be dealt with in a similar fashion to interior bearing walls. However, it is also important to know that when you cut an opening into an exterior wall to add a window or door, you are compromising the structural integrity of that wall. All outside windows and doorways are framed with smaller headers across their tops to support the roof. The rule of thumb in making structural changes is to assume that any change in the framework or roof structure of the house must be planned and executed by a professional. This work is also regulated by local building codes and may be subject to inspection.

Hidden Systems

The walls and ceilings of your home contain an array of wires, pipes, drains, and ducts. Planning to move or remove any wall or ceiling can mean uncovering and interrupting these utility systems. An expert can often predict what will be in the walls by following visible lines in the basement or attic as they enter and exit walls or ceilings. However, even the most inexperienced builder knows that you can never be sure what you'll find in a wall. Be prepared to deal with unexpected discoveries. Some will be problems, others entertaining surprises. When tearing a kitchen out in an older city home, we found a cache of photos taken during the construction of the home at the turn of the century. They showed a very different area in its infancy as a city and added to the owners enjoyment and knowledge of their home's history.

In the next few pages, we're going to offer a crash course in these hidden systems. It is not designed to enable you to work with them hands-on. That is best left to experts. It is designed to help you understand the potential problems and opportunities you'll face in coping with these vital sources of everything that makes your kitchen comfortable and functional.

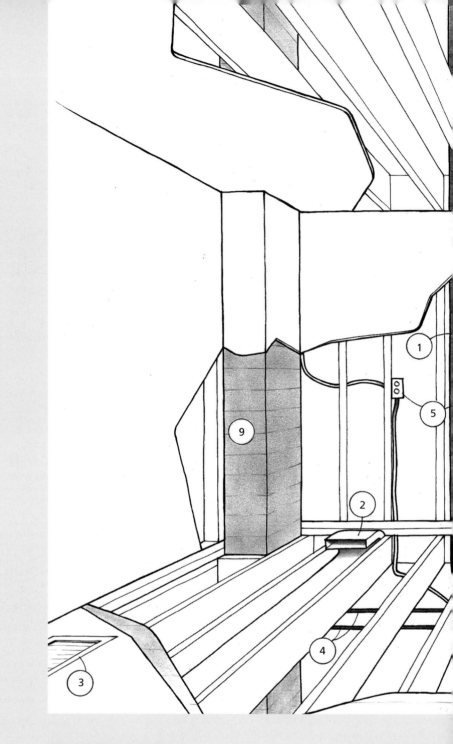

The Hidden Kitchen

Your kitchen is surrounded with framing, wires, pipes, ducts, and other hidden systems. These systems are essential to the function, comfort, and safety of not only your kitchen but also your entire home. Learning what they do and where they are is an important step in creating a new kitchen.

1. Drain pipes carry away water and waste. Vent lines pas vertically through walls and out the roof to eliminate suction in waste line.

2. Heat ducts rise from the basement and vent heat out through a cabinet base. In some cases,

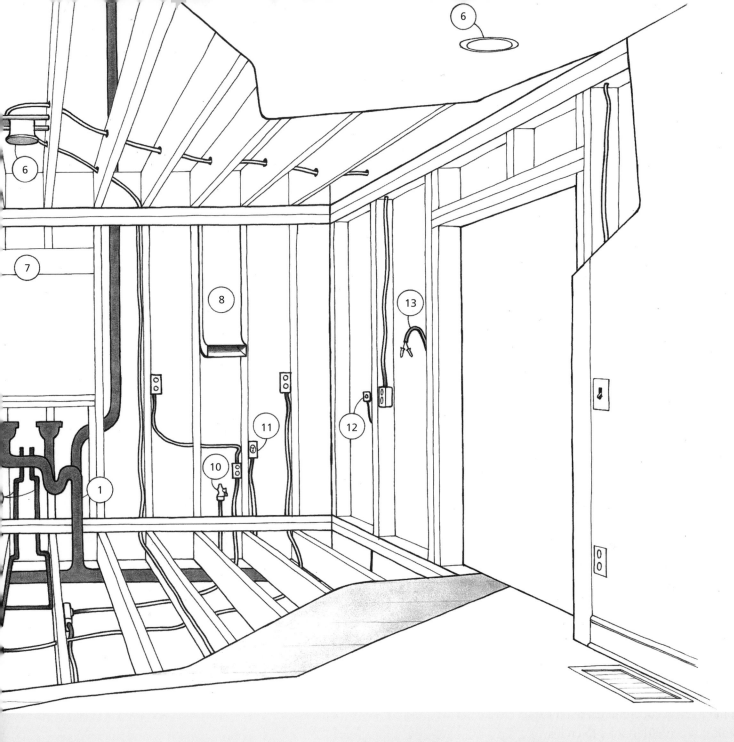

air-conditioning will run through these same ducts.

3. Cold-air returns allow cool air near the floor to flow back to the heating system.

4. Water-supply lines provide hot and cold water to sinks and appliances.

5. Electrical outlets and wiring provide a power source.

6. Recessed lighting is connected via wall switches and circuits for a variety of control locations.

7. A small header over the window takes up the load

from studs cut off to create the opening.

8. The duct for the range hood vents hot gases and odors outdoors.

9. The existing chimney must remain.

10. Natural gas lines supply gas to the range.

11. A 220-volt electrical circuit supplies high voltage to an electric convection oven.

12. A jack is the connection for the phone line and/or television cable.

13. Electrical wiring supplies electricity for an undercabinet halogen fixture.

ELECTRICAL

The electrical wiring system of a house has two main functions. It supplies outlets to provide power to a wide variety of appliances, and it powers and controls lighting built into the structure of the house. A house's wiring is divided into a number of circuits that start at a breaker box connected to the municipal power grid. These circuits spread out via wires into regions of the house where they are connected to outlets in boxes mounted in the walls, to built-in lighting in boxes in walls and ceilings, to switches, and directly into large built-in appliances.

The wiring diagrams, or schematics, used in residential construction are standardized, and any licensed electrician knows how to design an electrical system for residential use. Code requires that wires be run through walls and permanently affixed at certain intervals so they cannot be pulled out (see the photo at right). The heights that wall outlets and switches are placed at is determined by code and by common practice based on ergonomics. For example, wall switches are usually mounted at a standard height of 45 in. to be accessible to average-size people (see the illustration on pp. 52-53).

Kitchens use a lot of electrical power. Modern kitchens may have many dedicated circuits to ensure that there will not be too many high-wattage appliances on the same circuit. Common practice calls for every other outlet above a counter, for instance, to be on a different circuit. Large, power-hungry appliances usually have their own dedicated circuits. These appliances include refrigerators, micro-

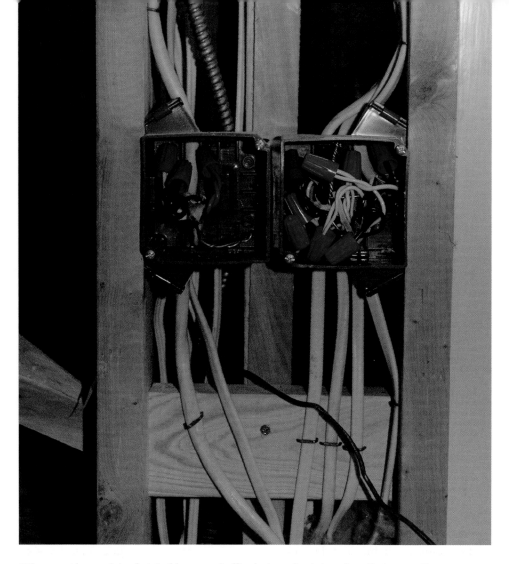

Wires must be run into electrical boxes and affixed at regular intervals so they cannot be pulled out.

waves, disposals, window air conditioners, and dishwashers. Generally speaking, any appliance that generates heat or cold will draw a lot of power and may require its own circuit.

Major electric appliances like ranges, convection ovens, and air conditioners may require 220-volt power, which is essentially two conventional circuits combined to provide a higher voltage. You must plan on having these special lines run before closing walls if your appliances require 220-volt supplies.

Other specialized users of power include computers and any appliance with an electronic memory, which is an increasingly common feature on so-called "smart" appliances like programmable VCRs and microwaves. These intelligent machines should be attached to surge protectors and/or power conditioners that ensure a steady flow of power free of damaging surges. Because so many homes are increasingly computerized and many local power supplies are inconsistent in their supplied voltage, we predict that many new homes and upgraded electrical systems will soon feature uninterruptible power supplies (UPS). UPS are devices that store power and then feed the correct voltage to the system in the event of a brownout. The supply lasts long enough for the users to power-down computers without losing any files.

The rule of thumb for upgrading all of these systems is overbuild while the walls are open. This is particularly true of your electrical system. We live in a time period characterized by unforeseen developments in technology. Providing for enough clean power now will prepare you for future innovations. Put in more circuits, more outlets, and more switching options, and run extra wires in anticipation of future upgrades.

Take a look at the lighting in your current kitchen. Most older kitchens suffer from inadequate or poorly planned lighting. When planning your new kitchen you have an opportunity to upgrade the lighting and to relocate switches and fixtures to more practical locations. In Chapter 6, we'll look at lighting design in more detail.

PLUMBING

Plumbing is more than just the pipes that bring in hot and cold water to your sink. It's a complex system designed to both supply and remove water and waste from your home. Plumbing installation requires specialized skills to ensure that water flows safely, quietly, and efficiently. It is essential to plan any upgrades early because most of the work must be hidden in the walls of your new kitchen.

Supply lines Plumbing lines come in two types—supply and waste. They are very different in many ways. Supply lines bring hot and cold water into your kitchen from the hot water heater and main water-supply line. They are pressurized by water pressure provided by the water authority or, if you use spring or well water, by a pumping system. The fact that these lines are pressurized is important because it determines what they are made of and because pressurized lines require extra care in their installations to avoid leaks.

Supply lines are made of copper, plastic, or galvanized steel. Older galvanized steel lines clog up over time from mineral deposits and eventually must be replaced by copper or plastic, which do not. If you own an older home with galvanized-steel supply lines, have them replaced now because they will eventually become useless. You may notice a corresponding increase in water pressure as a result of the change.

The quality standard in supply lines is copper pipe soldered together at the joints. In some areas, plastic or polyvinyl-chloride (PVC) supply lines are allowed by code. They are cemented together with a solvent-based adhesive, which permanently bonds the joint. Given the choice, most plumbers will recommend copper for its durability and strength over plastic. Copper lines are much quieter than plastic and less susceptible to damage. In our opinion, you should install the best plumbing supply lines you can afford. They should last the life of your home. In many areas, building codes still require the use of copper supply lines.

Supply lines must be provided for all sinks, dishwashers, refrigerators with ice makers, and any other fixed appliance that uses water. Plumbers have quite a bit of flexibility in running lines because the water pressure will push the water through complex corners and joints with no problem. However, all plumbing occasionally entails drilling holes in wall studs and floors or cutting away framing. By planning your plumbing needs carefully, your carpenter can anticipate these needs and build in spaces to run pipe without compromising the structural integrity of your house.

Waste lines Supply lines bring plenty of water into your kitchen. But all that water has to go somewhere after it is used, and that is down the drain and into the waste water system, eventually finding its way into sewers or a septic system. Waste lines are not under pressure, so they do not require the same degree of leak protection as supply lines. Because waste water often contains solids, these pipes are larger, up to 6 in. in diameter, and made of brass, copper, cast iron, or plastic, which is acceptable in most areas.

Waste lines must have a steady downward flow to drain properly. Without pressure to push the water through the system, they rely on gravity to keep things flowing. For this reason, they require more planning to travel around obstacles than supply lines. You need a waste line wherever you have a water supply, and every waste line must have a curved trap with a small quantity of standing water in it below the drain. This trap keeps sewer gases including methane

Plumbing can be found almost anywhere in a building. These pipes are all that remain of an old island and will be relocated.

from flowing up the drains and into the rooms. The trap must either have a removable clean-out access point for unclogging it, or it must be easily disassembled. The main waste lines must also have clean-out access at various points in the system.

Vent lines Waste lines do not just go down. They also go up and out of the roof of the building to vent out gases and to eliminate suction, which could empty water from traps and prevent drains from draining properly. These vent lines are often overlooked by neophyte designers and amateur plumbers with potentially disastrous results. Every drain must have a corresponding pipe running up and out to the outside to eliminate suction. A system without a source of outside air can suck water out of the traps, allowing sewer gases into the house. These vent lines run in your walls and up to the roof. They branch off of the waste lines at places near the trap within a distance determined by local code. An improperly designed vent system will result in poor drainage and foul-smelling, potentially hazardous gases entering the house.

Vents are a major design consideration because they affect your choices in placing sinks and other water-using appliances. You cannot simply add a vent line anywhere you want because it must go up to the roof. This venting becomes a particular problem with sinks located in islands and peninsulas, where there is not a convenient wall to run your vent pipe into. Because you don't want a vertical vent pipe running up and out of your island, plumbers have devised complex systems for routing vent pipes off of islands. It is not a job for an amateur and will increase the cost of placing a sink in an island as opposed to against a wall near an existing stack. All vent systems must conform to local plumbing codes.

WATER PURIFICATION AND SOFTENING

A clean source of pure water is vital to good, healthy cooking. With many areas suffering from poor municipal water quality you should consider installing a water-purification system or a water softener. This is another choice to be made at the planning stage, unless you install the system in the basement to purify the entire home's water supply.

GAS

Many cooks prefer gas as a fuel because of its open, clean flame and instant heating ability. If you choose gas-powered appliances, either propane or natural gas depending on your location, you'll need to have black-iron threaded gas pipes run into each appliance's location. Like all piping, these pipes are rigid, heavy, and must be worked through walls and floors. Installation must be done by a qualified installer. A leak is life threatening and could result in death and/or the destruction of your home. Properly installed, gas is very safe and burns cleanly.

Gas is pressurized by the supplying utility company. However, many restaurant-style stoves with high-BTU burners and broilers will not work up to their potential on the normal gas pressure supplied to your home. Restaurants typically have larger commercial gas lines that deliver higher pressure, resulting in the fast, high heat that characterizes restaurant-style cooking. If you want this blast of heat, check with your appliance manufacturer for the stove's pressure and gas-line requirements and with your gas company to see if you can get the pressure you need. And check to make sure they're compatible before you buy these expensive appliances.

HVAC

Heating, ventilation, and air-conditioning (HVAC) are typically installed and serviced by the same technicians. Planning for your HVAC requirements is part of planning the airflow in and out of your kitchen. As we saw in the last chapter, besides heating and cooling a room, good airflow makes the room feel better, removes odors and gases, and tends to make the space a much more comfortable environment to work in. In fact, you should think of these systems as the environmental climate-control part of your kitchen design.

Heating Heating comes in several forms, including forced-air systems that use two sets of ductwork—one for hot air coming out of the furnace and the other to return cold air to the furnace for reheating. This complex ductwork takes up a lot of space and often runs through kitchen walls on its way

to other rooms. Moving or removing a wall usually means rerouting a duct, which can be tricky because of the clear, open, straight runs of space they require. Forced-air systems are easily fitted with central air-conditioning units that can share their ductwork system for summer cooling.

Steam or hot-water heat uses a system of pipes and radiators that circulates steam or hot water, which in turn heats the air in the room. The heat is very even but doesn't heat up or cool down as quickly as forced air. These systems are preferable for allergy sufferers because they don't blow dust and pollen particles around. They require considerable piping, entailing yet another set of pipes snaking in and out of your walls. Radiators and baseboard units come in a wide variety of styles and shapes, but they still require a certain amount of wall space to function properly. These systems are closed loops operating under pressure. As a result, you cannot simply move a radiator and hook it up to the system again. The entire system must be flushed out and reassembled by an experienced heating contractor for proper operation after any change. If you have a steam or hot-water heating system, you won't have an existing duct system to use for central air-conditioning, making it necessary to install one.

Electric heat is easy to install, easy to locate, and only requires electrical circuits to be run into the heater's location, which makes remodeling easier than the other systems. However, electric heat is very expensive to use and offers no ducting possibilities for central air-conditioning.

A popular heat system for new construction is an in-floor heating system, which is a complex of tubing set in concrete beneath your flooring. Warm water circulates through the tubing, resulting in quiet, even, energy-efficient heat. This system must be installed early in the construction process, and care must be taken not to break into the system with nails or other construction fasteners. Again, it does not provide a cooling component.

In addition to ductwork or plumbing, heating systems require a low-voltage thermostat for temperature control wired to the furnace. Thermostats today are sophisticated devices designed to control heating and cooling in several different rooms or zones in the household. You can program them to turn down temperatures at specified times to save on energy costs. Again, you may have to plan for a location for these control panels.

Air-conditioning Air-conditioning is becoming standard in new construction and is a necessity in many parts of the country. Besides providing cooling, it can dehumidify and clean the air, and it offers a benefit that is often overlooked: noise reduction (because windows are kept closed). In a busy urban environment, this reduction can be a significant benefit.

If you have an existing heating system that does not use ducts, you either must install ductwork for central air-conditioning or buy a window unit. A window unit is easy to install, but it may be noisy, it takes up window or wall space, and it may not cool the entire home. Central air-conditioning is quiet because the com-

pressor is usually located outside, away from the house, and it provides an even whole-house cooling and dehumidifying. Removing humidity is a big plus when doing a lot of cooking in a hot, closed environment.

Ventilation All of your HVAC systems may be enhanced by adding ventilation fans, good-quality ceiling fans, and other air-circulation devices. Cheap ceiling fans are not constructed to move a lot of air because their motors cannot handle the strain. They often do not make any appreciable improvement in airflow. Buy a good one, and remember that installing a quality ceiling fan requires an electrical box securely mounted to the framing of the ceiling, a power source, and special switching mounted on the wall.

A good ventilation system for removing cooking gases and hot fumes can vastly improve the quality of your kitchen. If you use a high-power range or ovens, you must have a powerful vent system that routes heat out of the house because these appliances generate large amounts of heat.

Cooking ventilation comes in several configurations. Down-draft vents surround a range at counter level and draw smoke and fumes down and out through the wall or floor. They have the advantage of not taking up space over the appliance. Overhead vents and range hoods come in all kinds of styles with varying efficiency, from low-priced hoods that ineffectually cycle air back into the room to large hoods that could suck a gale out into the outer environment. Both styles require ductwork to the outside and a power source.

COMMUNICATIONS TECHNOLOGY

In our information-driven environment, kitchens are becoming a central location for many new communications systems. Even if you're not fully online yet, you may want to plan on installing lines for additional phones, cable TV, computer networks, and audio and video systems. A television is a common kitchen appliance these days, and you may want to install a pair of stereo speakers above your cabinets or in your ceilings for music while working, relaxing, or entertaining. The time to do it is now.

We're seeing more computers in kitchens, particularly since recipes and cookbooks work well as multimedia productions. The day when you call up a Julia Child recipe on the World Wide Web or check the availability of exotic ingredients at your supermarket via the Internet is already here as we write these words. E-mail exchanges with family members and homework are all functions of kitchen computers, too. Plan a spot and a dedicated phone line for these new kitchen resources. Every kitchen has a phone and many households are adding additional lines for kids, fax machines, modems, and other uses. Fortunately, cordless phones mean we don't have to be tied to a wire, and they work particularly well in the kitchen.

SECURITY SYSTEMS

Security systems involve yet another set of wires in your home. These systems include motion detectors, electric eyes, smoke and carbon monoxide detectors, and a central system that calls the police in the event of an emergency. Even with today's wireless systems, you'll need access to phone lines, a place to locate control panels, and hard-wired ceiling boxes for detectors. A hard-wired box means that the detector is powered by normal household electricity rather than by batteries and is wired into the system like a ceiling light.

CHIMNEYS

In older homes it is not unusual to run into a brick or block chimney during demolition. Often these chimneys are no longer used, or they may be a part of the venting system for a furnace and hot water heater. If they still function as a chimney, they can't be removed without providing another way for hot gases to leave the house. Even if they are no longer used, removing them can be a dirty and complex job.

Often they are built into the structure of the house up through the roof, necessitating roofing and framing repairs and the removal of large quantities of masonry. Usually chimneys are simply designed around rather than moved or torn down.

The temptation exists to use these chimneys for a woodstove or to add a fireplace. However, unless they are in good condition and were built for these functions, it may be dangerous to do this. Consult a qualified mason or engineer before using them. If you want a fireplace or woodstove in your kitchen, you can always add a double-walled stainless chimney outside the building envelope.

Understanding the existing systems hidden in your kitchen is one of the first steps in the process of designing your new kitchen. Even if you are only making minor changes, you'll find that the more you know about the systems hidden in your walls, the less likely you will be to face expensive problems later. In Chapter 6, we'll look at these same systems as part of the design of your new kitchen.

Part Two

DESIGN AND STYLE

CHAPTER 5
Designing with the Physical Space

Creativity is a mystery to many of us. Somehow, when planning a project, we must go from the practical to the creative and back again. Designing your kitchen is no exception. You start with an existing or planned space, systems that must be worked with, and limitations of budget and time. You have a set of very real requirements for functionality, yet you want a final room that is aesthetically pleasing and comfortable. The combining of these practical and pleasurable concerns is the essence of the design challenge you face.

Creativity in design combines a practical step-by-step process with an intuitive set of choices that determine the final appearance and usefulness of your kitchen. In this chapter, we're going to show you a practical process for addressing both aspects of designing your kitchen. We'll go through the process of producing working scale drawings of your space now and as a potentially changed environment, and we'll start to look at how you can get in touch with the intuitive part of you that makes choices in color, light, and tactile surfaces. In Chapter 3, we looked at how traffic flows through and around your kitchen and suggested that you sketch out those traffic patterns. Now we're going to take the next step—getting a more exact working plan of your kitchen on paper.

Putting Your Kitchen on Paper

Now that you're in the design stage, it's time to create a series of measured drawings of your existing kitchen. You don't have to be a draftsman or an architect to do this; all you need is a simple floor plan to start with. In the next few pages, we'll walk through the process of putting your kitchen on paper and show you a more advanced example of how drawings can help to change your space for the better, before you spend a penny or swing a hammer. We'll start by making a measured sketch of your kitchen the way it is now.

MEASURE THE SPACE

If you're building a new home or adding a completely new wing to an existing one, the builder will have blueprints to work with. Get your own copies and use them to follow the process in this chapter. If you are remodeling an existing kitchen, you'll need to measure it and do a simple drawing with measurements.

Start by making a quick pencil sketch of the room from an overhead perspective. This floor plan doesn't need to be to scale, but it should include doorways and windows with a basic version of the other rooms and outdoor areas connecting to the existing kitchen. Then take your tape measure and measure the wall lengths between corners, windows, and doors.

(Buy a good-quality 25-ft. tape measure. You'll use it all the time.) Add these numbers in feet and inches to your sketch. Measure the width of door openings and window openings and add them to the sketch (see the illustration below). Then measure across the widest point of the room in both directions and add these measurements to your drawing. Finally, measure ceiling height and doorway height(s) and make a note of them on the margins of your sketch.

Your measured drawing need not be an accurate rendering of the room. A simple floor plan with measurements written in and the relationships between walls, corners, and doors and windows sketched in is fine.

Floor-Plan Sketch with Measurements

Start with a simple outline of the room, including open spaces for doorways and markings for window openings. Then measure the room and write in all measurements.

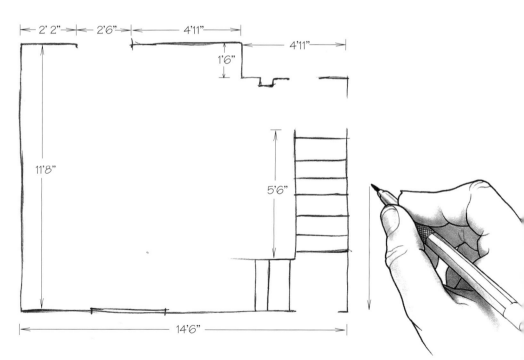

From Sketch to Scale Drawing

Now that you've measured your space, it's time to do a more accurate scale drawing of your floor plan. You'll need a large pad of graph paper ruled on ¼-in. squares and an architect's, or drafting, ruler, which you can buy at most art, office, or stationery supply stores. This ruler has the conversions in feet and inches to the scale of your graph paper printed on its three surfaces. It's an invaluable tool for thinking visually while maintaining a grip on the real space you have. Do your drawing in pencil because you'll probably make a few mistakes as you go. And buy a good-quality kneaded eraser while you're getting your materials.

Giving yourself plenty of space around the perimeter, start at one corner and begin drawing the outside edge of your space using the measurements on your sketch as a guide (see the illustration below). Make sure you choose a scale that will fit the entire room on your paper. For instance, most kitchens will fit on an 11-in. by 17-in. pad if you use a scale of ½ in. equals 1 ft. Draw a double line to indicate walls, and add more lines or leave a blank space at windows and doors. Sketch in a simple arc to indicate which way the doors open. If you have casement windows that swing open, indicate the range of their movement, too.

Once you've made the basic-outline scale drawing of the room, go out and get copies made. Have 15 or 20 done for various contractors to use and so you can try different schemes. You'll also want copies for various aspects of the job, such as cabinet layout or systems planning.

Basic Floor Plan Drawn to Scale

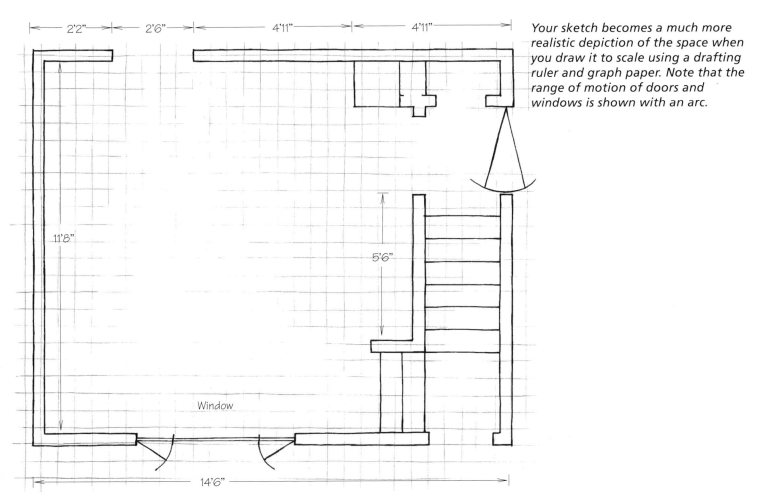

Your sketch becomes a much more realistic depiction of the space when you draw it to scale using a drafting ruler and graph paper. Note that the range of motion of doors and windows is shown with an arc.

LOCATE HIDDEN SYSTEMS

The next step is to add the various hidden systems covered in Chapter 4 to your scale drawing. Draw in sinks, stoves, built-in lighting, hot- and cold-air ductwork or radiators, chimneys, water-supply lines and drains, and any other existing fixed systems (see the illustration below). Locate wall outlets and light switches, indicating with a light line what fixtures they turn on and off. Add any other switches or control pads for alarm systems, ther-

mostats, garbage disposals, etc. Don't forget that dishwashers and refrigerators with ice makers have water lines attached. If you have any appliances that require 220 volts or natural gas lines, add them.

By now your scale drawing is getting pretty complicated. You've probably spent some time in the basement or in other rooms trying to figure out what pipe or wire goes where and why. As complicated as this may seem, it is much easier to build your new kitchen without expensive surprises if

you take the time to locate as many hidden elements as possible now. You won't get them all, but each one you uncover now can be dealt with on paper rather than when work is in progress.

When adding these systems to your drawing, it helps to use colored pencils with various colors for various systems, such as blue for cold water, red for hot, brown for drains, and yellow for electrical (see the illustration below). Get out the tape measure and try to approximate the actual locations

Existing Kitchen Elements and Systems

The wide range of things that must be considered in a kitchen begins to emerge as you add the existing elements and hidden systems to your scale drawing.

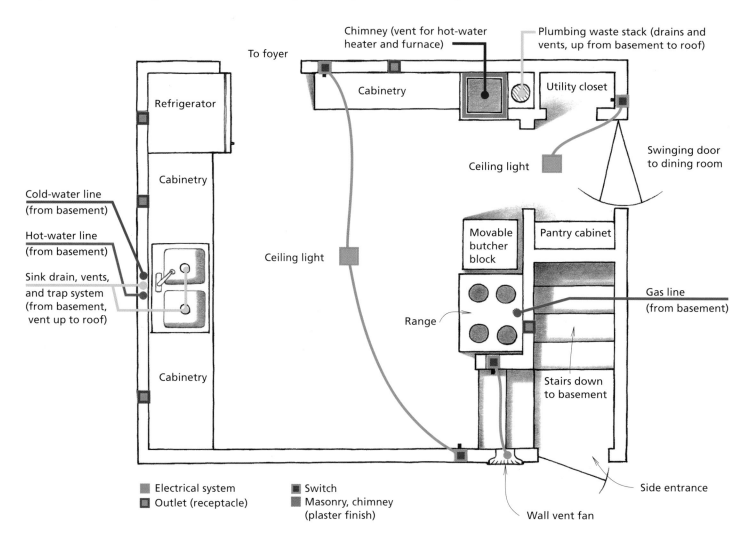

of each element. If your scale drawing is getting confusing with all this detail, make a set of drawings using copies of your originals and put systems on one, traffic flow on another, cabinets on a third, etc.

LOCATE ARCHITECTURAL ELEMENTS

Every house and apartment has various architectural elements that either function as structural components of the building or serve as a decorative or historical part of the home. These range from stairways to windows. It's important to locate and identify these elements so that you can make informed decisions about their future use or removal. As discussed earlier, moving a wall or a doorway after construction starts can have a serious impact on your budget and schedule. Take the time now to identify these architectural elements on paper before you consider moving or using them in your design. In Chapter 9, we'll be looking at using these elements in your final design to enhance your space, to maintain architectural integrity with the rest of the home, and to determine how your new kitchen will flow within the traffic patterns of the house.

IDENTIFY BEARING WALLS

Removing and relocating walls and widening openings in walls are often major aspects of both kitchen design and construction. The freedom to change the actual size and shape of the space you're working with can make the difference between a cosmetic refinishing of an existing kitchen and a truly functional improvement.

Before you can exercise freedom of choice architecturally, you have to identify what exists now and how it interacts with the rest of the house. Sometimes removing a wall involves nothing more than careful demolition; other times it involves re-engineering the building's structure to ensure integrity and safety. This is a good time to have a designer or contractor take a look at your space and help you determine which structural elements can be easily moved and which require more planning. With a professional's help, you can mark the nonbearing walls on your plan and identify any important considerations of the other walls, such as load and span, that will affect the decision to move or remove them.

EXPERIMENT WITH MOVING WINDOWS AND DOORS

On your scale drawing look at windows and doors, add in connecting rooms and outdoor areas, and then look at those connections along with the windows and doors and consider how moving, adding, or removing them might change the space for the better. You can increase both usable space and the spatial feeling of a room by using bay windows or a rectangular bump-out with windows on three sides. Doorways can be widened and opened up to the ceiling to make a connecting space more open and to add a sense of spaciousness to a room.

These connections must be respected during the design process. Changing them can mean a vastly improved space or one that impedes the natural flow of the household. Look at what you have now and play with other traffic patterns on your sketches until any potential improvements begin to present themselves.

IDENTIFY WORK AND CABINET SPACE

By now the potential storage, work, and appliance space has begun to define itself. When you leave room for people to move and room for doorways and windows, you have only a limited amount of space left to work with. Unobstructed wall space is a resource, as are wide areas of open square footage in the center or ends of the room. These resources must be carefully utilized and protected to keep the room functional and must be open enough to avoid a cramped feeling.

MAKE CUT-OUTS

At the minimum, your kitchen will contain: storage in the form of cabinets; pot racks or pantry space; appliances, including a stove, refrigerator, oven, sink, and dishwasher; work surfaces, including counters and islands; and social space. The social space may include seating areas and possibly a casual relaxation area. You may want a space for a desk or computer. Placing all of these minimal elements into your design will require much experimentation. So, in addition to your scale drawings, you may want to make

RESOLVING PROBLEMS ON PAPER: BEFORE AND AFTER

Overhead perspective drawings (done by architects or designers) can clearly show proposed solutions to design problems. In this example, we're looking down on the kitchen shown in the scale drawing on p. 65. Solid lines indicate the work triangles, and dotted lines indicate traffic flow. The "before" drawing below shows the kitchen before remodeling, and the "after" drawing on the facing page shows

how problems were resolved on paper before doing any demolition or construction. The problems and their solutions include:

• In the "before" drawing, the refrigerator (1) partially blocks the doorway, and the refrigerator door completely blocks access to the kitchen when it's open. In the "after" drawing, the refrigerator (1) is moved to the other end of the room and is replaced with a

wall of shallow cabinets, widening the entryway.

• At 2 in the "before" drawing, two doorways form a cramped pantry between the kitchen and the dining room. The solution (2 on the "after" drawing) involved removing doorways to create a continuous ceiling from the kitchen to the dining room. The old pantry cabinet was removed and a continuous run of shallow

"Before"

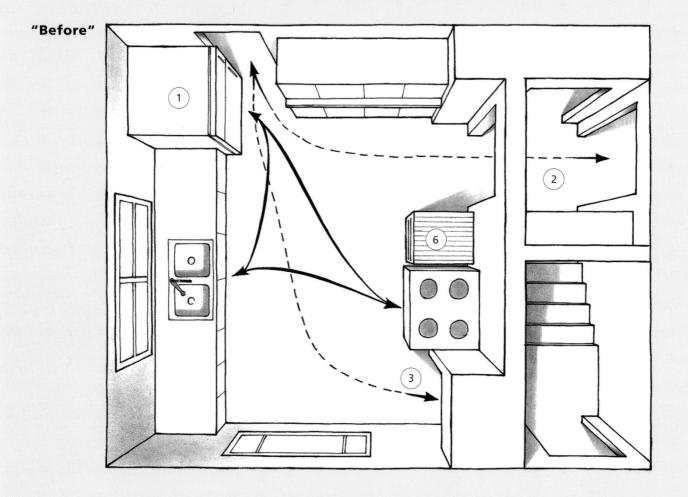

cabinetry and counter was installed in its place, widening the passageway. The new cabinetry now serves as a sideboard and bar area for the dining room.

• At 3 on the "after" drawing, a wall and doorway were removed to reduce congestion at the entryway, and at 4, upper cabinetry was installed to add storage. A peninsula counter (5) was installed to provide a small seating area and a place for food preparation, replacing the old rolling cart (6 in the "before" drawing).

• In the "after" drawing, the depth of the cabinetry is varied to provide wider passageways, and new floor-to-ceiling walls of cabinets replace the pantry's storage (7). These two solutions create more space, a high, airy ceiling for better light and airflow, and an improved traffic pattern for cooking and socializing.

Testing out solutions on paper means you can experiment freely without fear of making costly mistakes. If you are uncomfortable with this process or get stuck with one or more problems, consider taking your scale drawings to a professional designer for help. Often they can see solutions that elude you because of your preconceptions about the space.

"After"

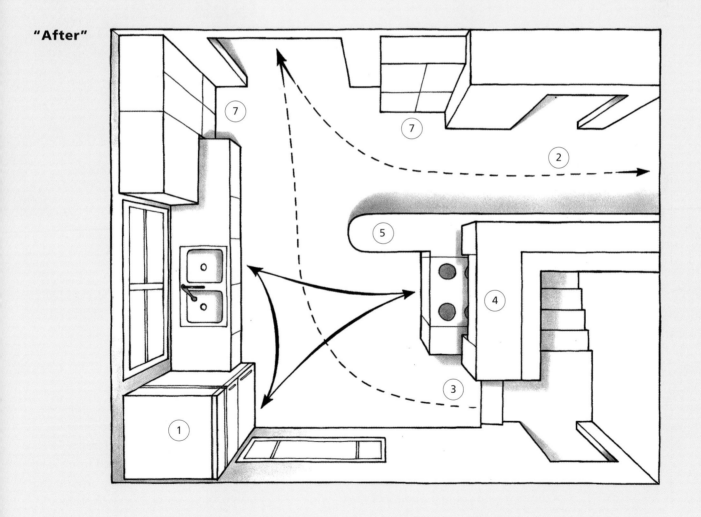

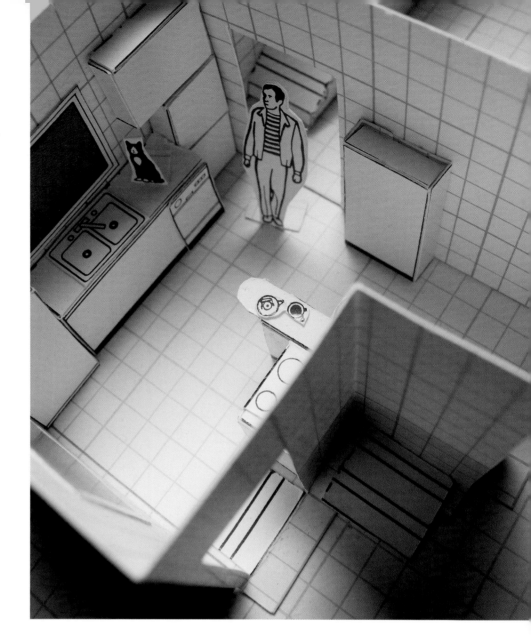

Design kits like this one are available to help you work with the space in your kitchen. Simple models can help you identify underutilized space, try out new window and door locations, and experiment with different cabinet and appliance layouts.

paper cut-outs of standard-size appliances and cabinetry, furniture, and any other elements. Or you can buy a kit or simple model if you don't want to make the pieces yourself (see the photo above). These cut-outs allow you to try out various arrangements on your measured floor plans.

Developing Your Design Resources

Creating a scale drawing of your kitchen is the first step in the design process. While you're working on your drawing(s) you'll want to start developing other design resources. These resources include tools like your camera and computer, research, and professional mentors to help you along the way. All of these resources, along with your drawings, will be-

come a part of an overall design file that you can draw on for ideas and inspiration.

"BEFORE" PHOTOS

Now is a good time to take snapshots of your existing kitchen to serve as both a reminder and a reference later on. Simply shoot each wall from as far back as you can get, going around the room. Take a few overall shots and some close-ups of any details you like or dislike. Many people skip this step and later regret it for several reasons. One, it's fun to compare "before" and "after" shots of your kitchen. Two, these photos may prove valuable during the construction process after you've demolished the old kitchen. They can provide clues about what happened to a pipe or wire you're looking for or a possible use for one that's just been found. And, if you're working with a designer, the photos can help them visualize your space while working on your design.

You'll be glad you took "before" pictures of your kitchen when you're trying to remember what the place used to look like. These are "before" shots of the kitchen on p. 24.

YOUR COMPUTER

If you have a computer, there are many home-design, CAD, and drawing programs available that can take your two-dimensional drawings and render them in three dimensions, making it very easy to try different structural or architectural changes (see the bottom photo at right). Some programs also feature walk-through functions that can actually walk you through your altered space. Because they require significant computer-processing power, these programs are just becoming available to consumers. If you can't use a CAD program at home, many kitchen cabinet dealers have programs that you can use. Just be forewarned: This service is a part of the sales process, and you may end up looking at walls of cabinets they hope to sell instead of the architectural elements that interest you.

YOUR DESIGN FILE

When you first considered creating a new kitchen, you probably started looking at kitchens in magazines, friends' kitchens, and kitchen appliances and cabinetry in stores. These things took on a different light as you

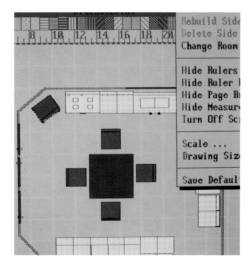

A computer makes it easy to try different arrangements of appliances and cabinetry. Consider any nonbearing walls movable, and don't limit your options at this stage.

started to consider the expense and what you liked or disliked about them. A large part of starting the creative process is this focusing of your attention on a previously unconsidered area. And early in the process it helps to gather information with an open mind as you discover available materials, play with color and texture, and research choices in everything from ranges to flooring.

For now, we recommend that you start assembling a design file of anything and everything that catches your

Your design file can contain anything that catches your eye or stimulates creativity. Don't limit what goes in at the beginning of the process, just start collecting ideas.

eye or contains information that might be relevant to your kitchen project. This file can be a folder full of photos and samples, a bulletin board filled with clippings, pictures, and swatches (see the photo above), or a box full of laminate chips, appliance brochures, and objects that have some relevance to your project. One project we worked on started with a photo from a magazine tacked to a refrigerator.

While the final kitchen bore little resemblance to the picture, it served as a source of inspiration and a reminder of the final goal during the deepest and darkest parts of the construction.

Your design file doesn't have to be limited to magazine tear sheets and manufacturers' samples. Sometimes a favorite photo, painting, or object can serve as a basis for the look of your

kitchen. One of the outcomes of starting a design file is that you start to build a coordinated palette of color, texture, and detailing choices, and you begin to see the relationships between these elements. Some choices will fit in well, and others may end up being taken out during the decision process. In Chapter 10, we'll look at a similar process based on using a favorite photo to pick textures and colors that evoke a certain feeling for your finished kitchen.

As we walk through the many steps in the design process, add notes and information to your design file. Even if you work with a designer or an architect, this file will serve as an invaluable resource, giving him a better idea of what appeals to you and of how you visualize using the finished kitchen. Don't limit what goes into the file, especially at the beginning. You'll find yourself subconsciously organizing and reorganizing the various ingredients as you go through the process.

PROFESSIONAL HELP

Now is an excellent time to get outside input. You've gotten far enough into the process to interact with a design professional if you choose (see the sidebar on the facing page). Often even a simple consulting arrangement at the design stage can mean innovative solutions and improved functionality because the designer or architect brings considerable experience to the project. Stay open to ideas while watching your budget, and you'll gain from the experience.

DESIGNERS AND ARCHITECTS

Coping with three-dimensional design is a time-consuming, creative process that requires a lot of work and experience. For many of us, it is very difficult to understand the potential of the space we have because we are not used to thinking in three-dimensional terms. Using a kitchen designer or an architect well versed in residential design can make a big difference in the overall success of your kitchen design. These professionals have the experience thinking in three-dimensional terms, and they have the creative tools necessary to break through existing concepts to come up with new and effective solutions.

Does using a design professional mean losing creative control? Every designer and architect we've talked with felt that the answer was a resounding "no!" Informed clients who know what they like and how they will use a space are a big help to a designer. Any professional design process starts with an evaluation of the goals and usage of the new space. This input comes from you and your lifestyle and budget. The more involved you are in the process (assuming you remain open-minded), the better your design will turn out.

Professional designers do not work exclusively on high-budget projects. While their compensation is often tied to the monetary scale of the project, you can hire them on a consulting or fee basis for smaller projects or to handle one or more aspects of your design, such as spatial design or detailing. Tell prospective designers up front what your budget and your goals are and then listen to their input. Often they know many ways you can get more for your money, which more than makes up for their fees.

Finding the right professionals means looking at their work, interviewing past clients, getting referrals, and checking out everything you would with any contractor. You may find a good designer at a cabinetry-oriented kitchen design store, but more often than not these "kitchen designers" are basically skilled salespeople. Interview them for their view on aesthetics and how they handle the overall design process, not just the cabinetry and appliances (their profit centers). Consider using them only if you feel they mesh well with your desires.

In the next chapters, we'll be looking at the various elements on your measured plans in detail from a design point of view. Read through and work on your scale drawing as you go. Add to your design file from as many sources as you can. As it fills up, you'll become more focused in certain directions and will start seeking specific information on the areas that interest you. The design process is well underway and will build momentum on its own until you're making final decisions on paint and housewares.

CHAPTER 6

Systems as Design Elements

The ancient Greeks defined the elements as water, fire, air, and earth, and to a certain degree these distinctions fit well with the kitchen-design process. The systems in your kitchen provide a flow of water, light, heat, cooling, and ventilation into, through, and out of your home. They are made of a wide range of materials, both man-made and natural. It is helpful when you begin to design your new kitchen to consider the elemental nature of these systems. Separately they provide water for cleanup, fire for cooking, warmth for comfort, and light for working; put together they create the overall environment and power source for all of the functions of your kitchen.

In Chapter 4, we looked at all the hidden systems you need to consider when beginning the design process. In this chapter, we're going to consider those systems as design elements in your new kitchen. These systems are not just obstructions or necessary parts of your kitchen; they determine to a great degree how your kitchen will function, both practically and on an aesthetic level. The choices are extremely broad, and gathering the information you need to make these choices is another important part of the planning process.

In this chapter, we're going to provide standard guidelines for placing items like electrical outlets and switches. We're also going to consider the various options available in choosing things like sinks and lighting. Your range of choice is very broad, and in order to keep from getting bogged down, you must narrow your choices based on budget and use.

Considering systems before cabinetry and counters is important because they are usually fixed in location during construction. Lines and wiring are run in while walls are open and lighting fixtures are installed. The location of items like sinks and ranges determines what kind of cabinets will be installed and where. And many of the visible elements of the systems like faucets and lighting have a strong effect on the overall style of the room.

Water

The sink is the central point of many kitchens. It serves as a water source, a cleanup area, and, with a disposal, a waste-removal site. It is connected to hot- and cold-water lines, drains and vents, dishwashers, disposals, and oth-

Sinks are more than just a source of water. They are a complete system, including sprayers, soap dispensers, and instant hot-water sources.

er appliances requiring a flow of water. Sinks are made of metal, ceramic, man-made resins, stone, and glass. In general, sinks perform a very basic function, but they can become complex tools in their own right.

In considering a sink, you have numerous options. Start with use. If you make regular use of a dishwasher for most of your cleanup, you may only require a single-well sink equipped with a sprayer for rinsing off waste and washing large pans. If you do a lot of dishes by hand, a large double- or

triple-well sink with an attached drain board will make this task much easier. Serious cooks with a large battery of commercial cookware may want a deeper sink with a powerful commercial sprayer. However, these deep sinks are hard on the back, and commercial pressure sprayers seldom keep their spray confined to the sink area, necessitating a commercial tile floor with built-in drains for cleanup.

In larger kitchens or kitchens with a well-defined separate area for entertaining or for a specialized function like baking, you should consider a second, smaller sink (see the top photo at right). A single-well "bar"-type sink comes in handy for making drinks or for rinsing utensils used during food preparation.

The material the sink is made of is the next consideration. Stainless-steel sinks are cost effective and easily cleaned. Buy a better-quality stainless-steel sink for its higher nickel content, thickness, and noise insulation, which are all factors that make a big difference in daily use. Glazed cast iron is another common choice because of the deep, durable colors that are available and the heavy, smooth weight that means a quiet, lifetime sink. Cast-iron sinks can scratch and should be cared for with nonabrasive cleaners.

Ceramic sinks are making a comeback, both as a surface over iron and as solid-material sinks (see the bottom photo at right). In Great Britain, large ceramic farm sinks that form their own section of counter are a popular retro look harking back to the '40s. They often come with wooden drain boards made of a naturally water-resistant wood, such as mahogany or maple. Be forewarned that any wood exposed to water will eventually discolor and lose its finish. For some tastes, this results in a desirable patina, for others an unappealing used look.

Recently, we've seen breakthroughs in sinks made of man-made materials, including composites containing minerals, resin sinks cast in high-tech plastics, and other stonelike materials. These sinks can be an integral part of a counter made of the same material, creating a seamless look that is easy to maintain. Stains can be sanded out, although some of these materials can burn or be etched by acidic materials. Sinks are also available in exotic mate-

A small second sink near this dedicated baking area increases the area's utility and saves the cook long trips across the room to rinse bowls and add water to recipes.

This ceramic sink features a removable cutting board with an opening to sweep trimmings through and into a disposal. Not only are the maple board and glazed ceramic sink functional, but they also offer an attractive combination of textures.

Sink-Mounting Options

A surface-mounted sink has a raised rim that seals against the top surface of the counter. It can be used with any counter material, including laminate.

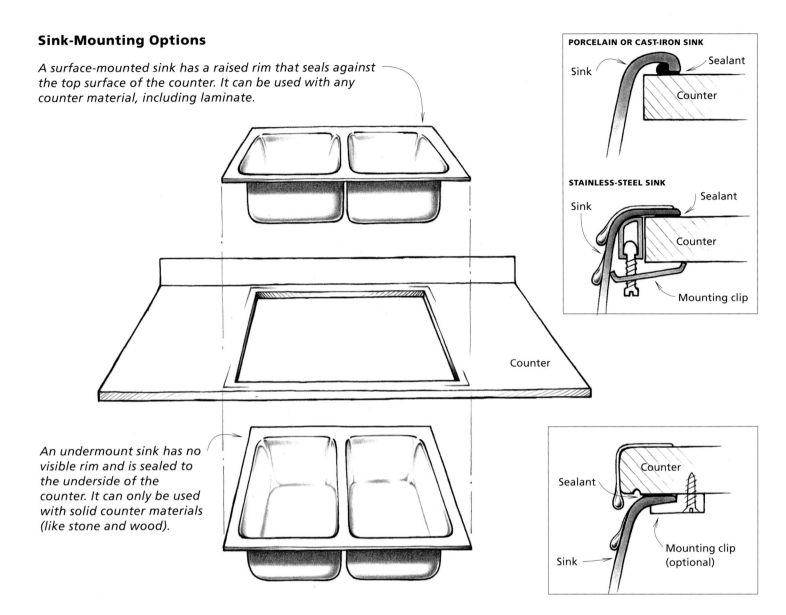

PORCELAIN OR CAST-IRON SINK

Sink — Sealant

Counter

STAINLESS-STEEL SINK

Sink — Sealant

Counter

Mounting clip

Counter

Counter

Sealant

Sink

Mounting clip (optional)

An undermount sink has no visible rim and is sealed to the underside of the counter. It can only be used with solid counter materials (like stone and wood).

rials, including nickel plate, gold plate, stone, glass, and other unusual materials. Carefully consider the expense, care, and cost of installation before choosing the more exotic materials.

SINK MOUNTING

Sink mounting offers a few options, chiefly surface-mount sinks and undermount sinks. Surface-mount sinks incorporate a raised rim that goes over the counter as the sink is dropped in from the top (see the illustration above). They require careful installa-

tion and caulking to keep water from running under the sink and delaminating or damaging the counter underlayment.

Undermount sinks are a recent innovation offering a streamlined appearance and the advantage of allowing water to run off the counter into the sink. Because the counter edge is potentially exposed to water, solid counter materials are a necessity around undermount sinks. Also, because these sinks must be mounted to the counter surface before the coun-

ters are installed, replacing them may mean removing and possibly replacing the counter.

FAUCETS AND ACCESSORIES

You have a wide range of choices for faucets and sink accessories. Faucets are something you use daily with several moving parts. For this reason, you should spend the money to buy a high-quality faucet even if you're on a restricted budget. This is not the place to cut corners because you'll end up paying again and again for break-

The space under a sink can be crowded with drains, supply lines, disposals, and water purification systems. Pull-out trays can help you get the most out of this limited and hard-to-reach space.

downs and leaks. A handsome, well-functioning faucet is one of those vital details that can lift a basic kitchen up into the realm of a better kitchen. It is something everyone uses and appreciates daily. If you use a dishwasher, consider a sprayer a necessity.

WATER SYSTEMS

If you live in an area with hard or unpleasant-tasting water, you might want to consider a water purification/softening system. Access to pure, clean water was once considered the norm, but increased demand and pollution have meant that more water supplies are tainted coming into the house. Water-conditioning systems can be installed to filter and remove minerals, resulting in less soap and mineral build-up, better taste, and safer water. These systems can treat all the water in the house or just in one area. The household systems are usually in-

stalled where the water line enters the house and all water runs through it. Area systems may be mounted under or near a sink and only treat the water going to that source. If you require an area system, consider the space and plumbing required before planning sink and cabinetry sizes.

Another item often installed under the sink is an on-demand hot-water supply. This system takes water from the supply, heats it as required, and feeds that water to a special faucet mounted on the sink. The water is hot enough for hot drinks and may be a safety hazard for families with small children. Again, a power source is required, and the sink you choose must have the required holes to accept the necessary faucets. Some stainless-steel sinks may be drilled or punched for this, but all others must have factory-supplied knock-outs for all sink-mounted accessories.

Heat Sources for Cooking

Ranges, cooktops, and ovens require power sources, principally natural or propane gas or electricity. From a design perspective, both gas and electric ranges are similar in appearance and function. The choice is based on the availability of the utility in your area and on your personal preferences. However, that decision may very well be determined by access to gas lines because gas lines require more care and accessibility during installation than a flexible electric wire that can be snaked through a wall.

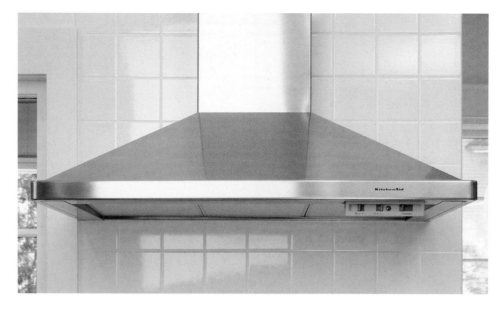

Range hoods not only provide the ventilation required by high-BTU stoves, but they are also important design elements because of their size, shape, finish, and visual impact.

Air: Heating, Cooling, and Ventilation

Fresh, clean air is a necessity in a kitchen, where cooking odors, heat, and waste all contribute to an atmosphere that must be vented out of the house. This ventilation becomes a design consideration because the vents themselves can represent a considerable presence in the budget and the room, often contributing architectural interest along with function (see the photo above). In kitchens featuring restaurant-style high-BTU ranges, proper ventilation is a necessity because of the tremendous heat their burners generate.

Heating and cooling systems don't materially affect design decisions except where a large radiator or vent must be visible. Fortunately, there is a very large selection of radiators and vent systems available in many colors and styles. You may have to search your area to find sources or go to national suppliers, but it's worth it to be able to replace a clunky and noisy radiator with a well-designed modern counterpart. Even if you're creating a period kitchen, consider upgrading existing visible elements of these systems to improve the function and appearance of your kitchen. And there are safety issues involved in using old radiators. Homes with small children should plan on building protective coverings for these large, hot objects or on upgrading to a baseboard system that has its own integral enclosure.

Light

We think well-designed lighting contributes more to the function of your new kitchen than any other system. It can focus on work areas for excellent visibility, or it can set a mood through-out the social areas. Good lighting can make a small kitchen seem bigger and a large one more intimate. It need not be expensive as long as you plan early for every option so the required wiring, fixtures, and switches can be built in during construction.

Lighting comes in three categories to offer you a wide range of choices. General lighting lights the overall space, usually from overhead, with a range of light spread around the room. Task lighting lights a specific work area with a clear light focused on the task at hand. Accent lighting creates and varies mood, lights decorative areas or artwork, and washes walls. Working together, these three types of lighting are a far step forward from the old overhead fluorescent or single light bulb fixture of the past (see the illustration on p. 82).

GENERAL LIGHTING

General lighting consists of natural light and high overhead lighting—either recessed, track, or ceiling-mounted fixtures—that provide an overall light source for the whole room (see the photo on p. 84). Plan on putting your general lighting on high-quality dimmers that are easily accessible from all entrances and exits. This access is required by electrical code in most areas.

General lighting shouldn't be limited to one central fixture. In fact, central overhead fixtures often result in shadows being cast on everything as you move around the room. A range of lights around a perimeter works better and need not cost more, as long as you plan the installation early in the design process.

Above: *The combination of general, task, and accent lighting allows you to customize your kitchen's environment for different times of day and social events.*

Right: *Task lighting focuses light on work areas. This unobtrusive halogen undercabinet lighting eliminates shadows cast by the person working in the space.*

Range of Light

The three forms of lighting—general, task, and accent—work together to enhance function, to create mood, and to provide a dramatic environment. Installing a mix of lighting types ensures complete flexibility in the future.

1. General lighting—ceiling fixtures and daylight
2. Task lighting—recessed floodlights
3. Task lighting—undercounter halogens
4. Accent lighting—low-wattage sconces

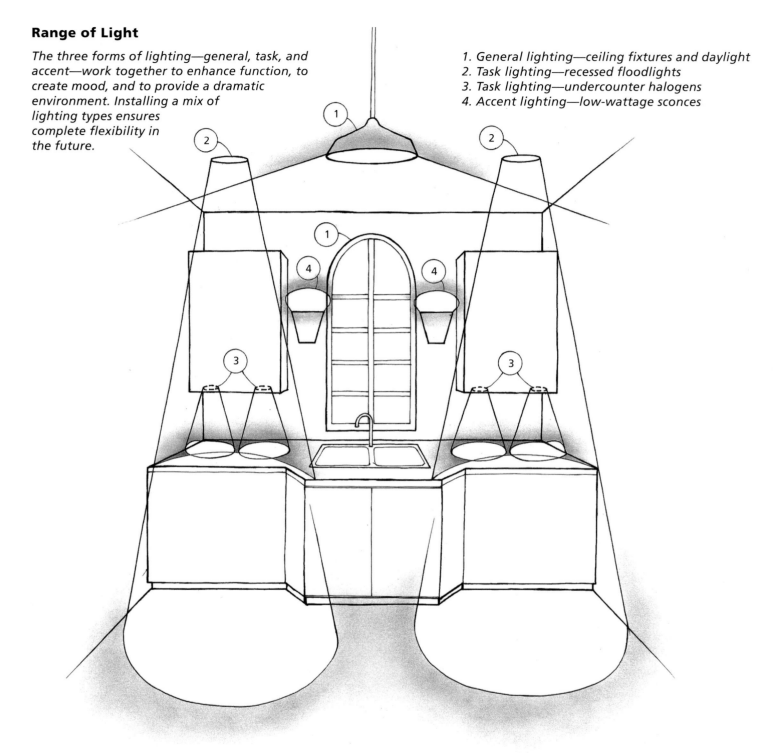

TASK LIGHTING

Task lighting is designed to focus light on counters and appliances, under upper cabinets, and inside appliances like ovens and refrigerators. Halogen fixtures provide a sunlike, natural, bright light that shows food off well and prevents eye fatigue that may accompany fluorescent light. Halogen is widely available as bulbs or in special low-voltage fixtures. It can be installed as recessed ceiling lighting, undercabinet lighting, or in the form of ceiling tracks or strips. The goal in planning your task lighting is to focus a bright wash of light onto work surfaces so that the person working does not obstruct the light, casting shadows. Task lighting may also use incandescent lamps to provide focused light, such as

Hanging lamps can serve as both general and task lighting, depending on their construction and location.

floodlights or spotlights. Both halogen and incandescent lamps provide a warm color balance well suited to lighting food.

ACCENT LIGHTING

Accent lighting contributes to the ambience, or mood, of the room. It is often focused on works of art, or it washes walls with a soft light that is not directed at anyone in the room. Preferably placed on dimmers, accent fixtures may be low voltage and have a number of small bulbs spread around to highlight architectural drama. Accent lighting contributes to the social mood of the room and, when combined with general and task lighting, gives you a very wide range of choices to customize your lighting environment. Often accent lights such as sconces become design details that pull the room together.

We generally recommend the use of dimmers on all kitchen lighting so you can vary your light's intensity during the changing day. Cheap dimmers

Large windows in the dining area are a source of general lighting, bringing natural light into this kitchen.

hum and generate radio frequency (RF) noise that affects radio and stereo reception. The better dimmers are quiet and allow you to preset favorite levels so you're not always sliding a switch around.

It's important to explore the full range of available fixtures before selecting your lighting. You may have to ask your local lighting-supply houses for catalogs to see the full range of recessed, track, and hanging fixtures available. Many of these fixtures feature striking designs and may become a dramatic part of your overall look. Avoid skimping on lighting because it can be costly to upgrade later after construction is completed.

Electricity

Kitchens require many electrical outlets for the numerous appliances used regularly. Because many of these appliances draw considerable power, particularly those with heating or cooling elements, your electrician will install numerous circuits dedicated to the kitchen alone. Standard practice is to have every outlet above a counter on alternate circuits with its neighbors. Large appliances like stoves and refrigerators will have their own circuits to prevent a dimming effect when they're turned on. Computers should be on a circuit with both surge protection and an uninterruptible power supply that temporarily maintains steady power during a brownout, allowing you to save any files open during the power interruption. (For more information on electrical circuits and wiring, see Chapter 4.)

It is better to err on the side of excess when installing electrical systems in your new kitchen. Numerous circuits will prepare you for the next wave of appliances and automation. Outlets over work surfaces should appear every 24 in., and islands should have their own dedicated outlets to avoid draping cords around the room.

As noted earlier, the location and wiring of switches can make a big difference in the function of the room. Switches must be easily accessible and should not be hidden behind doors or around corners. Preferably, switches should be located near all entrances and should be wired so that you can turn lights on and off from each entrance and exit. In order to avoid having a confusing array of switches in one location, plan on having different lighting accessible from different locations. This way anyone entering a darkened room can turn on some kind of lighting from any entrance without the confusion of five or six switches.

Detailing is vital to any successful design, and your choice of switch styles and electrical plates makes a difference in the overall ambience of the room. Stay consistent with the style, material, and color throughout the kitchen when choosing these details. A consistent approach helps pull together the overall look of the room and provides a recurring motif that can be carried into other detailing like door pulls or other hardware. For instance, if you choose brushed stainless steel as a hardware material, you can visually link the electrical plates, drawer pulls, and doorknobs by using the same finish on all. Even if they vary in style, the uniform finish can make them work well together.

Sound

Sound design is an element that many designers overlook. By sound design we mean the things you do to control sound in your environment. Anyone with a house full of active kids knows how much sound they can generate. Add in appliances and a television or stereo, and you have a lot of noise in your environment.

Excessive sound levels are fatiguing, cause stress, and offer a potential for hearing damage. Most kitchens have many square feet of hard reflective surfaces that contribute to the cacophony of a busy room. Balancing these hard surfaces with soft absorbent ones like upholstered furnishings, area rugs, and curtains can help reduce ambient sound levels by reducing the reflected sound in the room.

Sound escaping the kitchen into other rooms, particularly overhead into bedrooms, can also be a problem. Solutions include installing insulation in joist spaces before the ceilings or walls are installed and using double thicknesses of drywall or other wall materials. Alternating a dense wall surface with a soft-fill interior stops sound waves from passing through to other rooms.

This is also effective for reducing outside noise. In city environments or near busy roads, outside sound can contribute to a stressful environment at home. If you're replacing windows, ask for the sound transmission coefficient (STC) of the window and get those with the highest STC you can afford. These high-STC windows are usually double-glazed and more energy efficient than standard windows, yielding additional benefits for the extra dollars spent. Quilted blinds that are specifically designed to block sound transmission are also available.

These systems and the appliances they are connected to help create a comfortable and functional kitchen. Good lighting, ventilation, and newer kitchen technologies like audio-visual systems work together to make the environment you work in both safe and aesthetically pleasing. In the next chapter, we'll look at the appliances and the technology that serve as the working "front ends" of these systems.

CHAPTER 7

Appliances and Kitchen Technology

Your kitchen is a room filled with sophisticated tools designed to improve the quality of life on many levels. Appliances represent a significant investment of as much as one-third to one-half the cost of your whole project. Not only are appliances a major budget item, but they also should fit in with the overall kitchen design from both an aesthetic and a functional point of view. Appliances are anchors in the functional layout of any kitchen. They also attract the eye with their finishes and technology. The range of choices is staggering, limited only by budget and space. Fortunately, appliances have seen so many design improvements in the last decade that even the most basic kitchen budget doesn't mean compromising function or style. And, if you have the money and desire, you can equip your kitchen with the best of appliances and technology, from an eight-burner restaurant stove to a multimedia entertainment system.

But before you head out to the nearest appliance or electronics store, it's important to consider each purchase from a design viewpoint. This means looking at how you will use your purchases, how they fit into your space, how to choose the best model for your budget, and how they will look in your finished kitchen.

Choosing Appliances

There are three criteria to consider in choosing each appliance: functionality, budget, and style. Function choices are based on how you use that appliance and how often. For example, if you rarely do more than heat a meal in a microwave, you probably don't need a restaurant range.

Budget choices in appliances vary from a simple range starting at a few hundred dollars to a European commercial "cook's station" selling for five figures. All of the appliances we look at in this chapter are available in basic, mid-level, and high-end price ranges. The most important thing to keep in mind is that you must consider the overall cost of the appliance, including applicable taxes, delivery, installation, and required changes in your plans, such as outside venting and special gas lines. It may also mean making sure you can fit the appliance through the doors of the finished room.

Style and aesthetic choices are equally broad. Colors, materials, and design are all important to how your kitchen feels and looks. You can order every appliance from the same manufacturer in the same finish and look, or you can assemble an eclectic collection based on personal preference and function.

It's important when you shop for appliances that you educate yourself about the range of options. Unless you live in a major metropolitan area, it is unlikely that your local appliance dealers have more than a few brands and models on display. This occurs because of the high cost of carrying inventory and because the average consumer simply walks in and buys what he sees. It also comes about because styles and models change frequently. Your best bet is to ask for catalogs or send away for them. Look at several manufacturers' lines. If you're working with a kitchen designer, make sure you're not limited to lines the designer represents. Through this research you may discover a better choice for your needs at a better price. It also helps you make an informed decision about a tool you'll be using on a daily basis for years to come.

Ranges, Ovens, and Cooktops

On their most basic level, kitchens are about preparing and cooking food. This process requires a heat source. Today, we utilize a whole range of sources, from a plain cooktop burner to exotic heat sources designed for grilling, broiling, browning, and almost any other way of applying heat

to food. Your choice should be based on how often you cook, how complex those meals are, and how many people you will cook for. The style of food you regularly prepare may also affect your decision. If you use a wok regularly, for instance, you'll want at least one high-BTU burner that your wok and/or its supporting ring can fit on.

Ranges are one-piece units incorporating a cooktop and an oven. They can be freestanding, built-in, or a hybrid that slides in and appears to be built-in (see the top right photo on the facing page). Cooktops are units that drop into your work surface (see the bottom right photo on the facing page). They contain burners and sometimes inserts for grilling and other functions. They are usually matched with a separate oven or ovens.

Fuel choices include gas with open flames, electric heating coils, or electric halogen elements. Gas offers instant heat, a wide range of control, especially in the hotter temperatures, and is very fuel efficient. Electric coil burners are slower to heat and to cool but can be very good for low-heat simmering. Halogen burners are sealed flush with the cooking surface and heat instantly. They are very easy to clean and have a modern high-tech look as they glow orange under a tempered-glass surface.

Ovens are available with the same fuel choices, but electricity is often the preferred fuel because of its more exact temperature control and even heat. Some ranges offer a dual-fuel feature with gas burners on top and an electric oven below, combining the best of both uses of fuel. Many quality ovens offer a convection feature, which is a fan that circulates hot air

Above: *Slide-in units like the one above combine the look of a built-in with the ease of installation of a freestanding range.*

Left: *Commercial ranges are now made for home use, but they still require a significant investment in ventilation systems to vent heat and hot gases outdoors.*

Modern cooktops are shallow enough to allow for easily accessible drawers underneath, offering an excellent storage space for utensils or spices.

around food, yielding faster and more even baking. Be aware that convection ovens may be smaller inside than conventional ovens. (A tape measure may save you from discovering that your new oven can't handle a 20-lb. turkey on Thanksgiving morning.) If you have the space, using a separate oven and cooktop allows you to mount ovens in cabinetry at a height that is much more practical than the undercounter height found in one-piece ranges.

Finishes on most appliances are baked-on enamel, glass, or stainless steel. We are starting to see more plas-

tic surfaces on appliances, too, but not on those that come in contact with high heat like ranges. In a range, material construction is very important because of the high heat, the greasy nature of many foods, and the corrosive properties of many hot foods. The stainless-steel surfaces found on most commercial appliances are there because the harsh cleaning solutions and high heat found in restaurants won't hurt them.

In general, a less expensive range or cooktop will generate less BTUs of heat. Serious gourmet cooks know

Above: *Many refrigerators are now available in depths that fit in with standard cabinetry, which makes it easier to integrate them visually into the overall layout.*

Left: *This microwave is mounted in the custom cabinetry, raising it to an easy-to-reach level and freeing up counter space.*

that the high heat levels offered by commercial ranges are an important part of *haute cuisine* cooking techniques. High-heat burners sauté quickly, sealing in flavor, and boil large amounts of water very quickly. On the down side, you must have adequate venting to remove the enormous amount of heat from the kitchen. Also, if you are considering a commercial range, include the price of commercial-quality cookware in the overall cost. High-BTU burners can destroy inexpensive pots and pans.

Recently, we've seen the emergence of hybrid range designs that combine the best characteristics of commercial ranges with the size and budget limitations of the home kitchen. These hybrids are smaller, generate reasonable amounts of heat, are constructed of durable materials, and look like their professional counterparts. What they don't have are the enormous fuel requirements, blast-furnace environment, and stiff price tags we associate with real restaurant ranges.

MICROWAVE OVENS

The size and location of your microwave is dependent on what you use it for. If you primarily heat up leftovers, locating the microwave near an eating area makes sense. A baker might locate a small microwave near a preparation area for tasks like melting butter. The current generation of microwaves is smaller and often comes with hardware for mounting under upper cabinets (see the left photo above). Most cabinetry can be adapted for built-in microwaves.

Refrigerators

Refrigeration was the biggest technological breakthrough in kitchens in the twentieth century. Prior to reliable home refrigeration, the cook shopped every day and had to use all the perishable ingredients each day. Now we can freeze food in quantities, store condiments, and keep fresh vegetables, seafood, and meats available in the refrigerator for impromptu cooking. The refrigerator is both a tool and a storage place. As a tool, it allows you to cool or freeze food as part of a recipe, to make cold drinks, and to have instant access to ice. As a storage place, it holds food and fits in with your cabinetry design.

Refrigerators use a lot of energy, although we are seeing major breakthroughs in energy efficiency because of design incentives offered by utility providers. Practically speaking, your choice of refrigerator should be based on the size of your family, the availability of fresh food, your shopping habits, and how you cook. Big families need large refrigerators. If you're a single person or a couple with grown children who are out of the house, there is little need for an enormous unit. All too often we find large commercial refrigerators with very little in them, chosen for their appearance more than any practical need.

If you buy in large quantities to save money, to feed a large family, or to be prepared for unexpected needs, you may need a large freezer. However, in most cases an inexpensive freezer can be placed in the garage or basement rather than in the kitchen.

Refrigerators used to be one color: white. Then we saw the introduction of colors like almond and green. Now

Most newer refrigerators can be customized with panel inserts to match cabinetry or other appliances.

many refrigerators are built to accept outside panels that can be made to match cabinetry or laminates (see the photos above). Not only do these panels allow you to disguise these large appliances, but they also make it possible to easily change the color and appearance of your refrigerator.

The other design breakthrough in refrigerators is the availability of different sizes and shapes. Until recently, refrigerators were a universal depth that often made it hard to build them flush with a row of shallower cabinetry. Now there are different depths

available and units made to fit flush with various-size cabinetry (see the right photo on the facing page). Refrigeration is also available in drawer units, undercounter and overcounter units, and other unusual configurations. This means you don't have to design around bulky refrigerators. Instead, you can choose one that fits into your overall plan and works as an integral part of the cabinetry and storage system.

Dishwashers

Dishwashers have become a must-have appliance in most modern kitchens. In the past, dishes had to be prerinsed and scrubbed before the they were put in the dishwasher to ensure thorough cleaning. But current dishwasher design incorporates integral hot-water heating and a garbage disposal to create a dishwasher that really cleans while disposing of small food particles. Interiors were once limited to enamel and plastic, but the recent trend toward restaurant function in home appliances has meant that many better dishwashers have stainless-steel interiors.

Dishwashers are built-in appliances that require a water supply and drainage. They mount under cabinetry and have doors that can be customized via inserts to match other surface treatments in the kitchen or to create a unified color scheme for appliances. Noise levels from dishwashers used to present a problem, but newer models are much quieter and can be programmed to run at times when they won't disturb anyone. Standard dishwashers are 24 in. wide, with smaller models available for areas with limited space or for use in a bar or dining area.

Waste Management

Formerly, waste management in the home meant taking the trash out to a can in the yard. Today it may mean using a trash compactor, recycling, composting, or using a garbage disposal. Planning waste management in your new kitchen means planning for each of these tasks. Even if your community isn't doing full recycling and you don't have a garden, your future is likely to include more rather than less waste management.

TRASH COMPACTORS

Trash compactors reduce waste and trips to the outside trash receptacles by compacting garbage and therefore producing less of it. Recent trends toward recycling and composting have meant a significant reduction in the amount of loose trash generated by the average household, making compactors less popular than when first introduced. If you generate a lot of trash, have a long trip to trash receptacles, or have limited space for trash collection, a compactor may prove useful. Otherwise, you might want to consider creating a recycling center dedicated to keeping your trash and recyclables organized and sanitary.

RECYCLING CENTERS

With a national trend toward recycling plastics, metal, paper, and glass, we've seen the introduction of recycling centers for home kitchens. These centers are a combination of functional storage fitting into your cabinetry and an organization center. Their advantages include easy separation and storage of recyclables without filling the kitchen up with plastic bins and bags. The chief disadvantage is that they require a lot of space, and the users must clean them regularly to eliminate smells and pests. Recycling centers can be assembled from available cabinetry inserts and combined with special cabinet boxes allowing tilt-out or pull-out bins for easy access (see the left photo on the facing page).

Manufacturers are developing home dishwashers with commercial features. This model has a stainless-steel exterior and interior and a large easy-to-grasp handle—features found on its commercial counterparts.

Above: *Small speakers can be mounted under cabinetry or in unobtrusive spaces without compromising sound quality. The metal construction of this model offers some protection from splatters and moisture.*

Left: *These pull-out recycling bins are available as hardware inserts for Euro-style cabinets. The bins are easily accessed from above, and the Euro-style doors swing open far enough to get full use of the space.*

COMPOST BINS

You can further recycle waste by composting vegetable trimmings and leftovers. Compost bins with air filters are available for use inside. It's common to store these bins under sinks, but you may want to plan a space for one near your food-prep area.

GARBAGE DISPOSALS

Disposals are mounted under the sink and attached to the main drain or, in the case of multiple-well sinks, under the well used for initial cleanup and food preparation. Disposals can be added after the kitchen is built, but installation requires power and a ground fault circuit interrupter (GFCI)-protected wall switch located away from the water source. This means

that if you think you'll want a disposal, you should have your electrician plan for it. Disposals come in various sizes and powers, and we can only recommend buying the most powerful one you can afford.

Communications Technology

The use of emerging technologies for communication, education, and entertainment in the home is expanding at a rapid pace. Wires can carry audio, video, and cable right into your kitchen. Phone lines carry online service for your computer and tell security companies if you have a break-in. A personal computer (PC) located near

your cookbook shelf may help you search databases for recipes, find sources for ingredients, and even provide instructional multimedia to teach exotic cooking techniques. Because kitchens are often the social center of the home, it is likely they will become the communications center of the home, too.

TV, AUDIO, AND VIDEO

As a work and social area, your kitchen is an ideal place to catch up on the news, watch cooking videos, or listen to music. Now is the time to consider where to locate your audio-visual components. Speakers can mount under upper cabinetry or on walls with special brackets (see the right photo above). It's best to keep them away from heat and moisture.

You may want to run speaker wire before the walls are closed in and then provide special speaker outlet panels for hook-ups. Cable TV wiring also needs to be run, and outlets mounted at likely spots.

Televisions that mount under upper cabinets are available, or you can purchase wall-mount brackets to put them on. Integral VCR/TV combinations make sense in the kitchen, where wires and components need to be kept clean and out of the way.

TELEPHONES

People spend a lot of time talking on the phone in the kitchen. This used to mean walking around with an extra-long cord stretched to the limit as you drank a cup of coffee or watched a pot. Fortunately, cordless phones have made using the phone in the kitchen much easier, and they have made it a lot easier to add a phone where you didn't have a line previously by simply leaving the phone in the room.

However, in these information-oriented times the phone and its connection to the house are more than just a way to chat with friends. Many homes have two or more lines coming in dedicated to home businesses and Internet connections for their computers. We also have answering machines, fax machines, and in-home offices, and the kitchen is a logical place for all of them, provided you have the room.

Locating a sit-down desk and telephone area away from the main traffic flow creates a quiet and clean area for communications and household management.

COMPUTERS

We are not yet seeing dedicated kitchen computers or multimedia systems, but it is only a matter of time before specialized systems become available. Until that time your PC may be useful, but it will require its own area and that means planning extra cabinetry, work surfaces, electrical sources, and space.

Designing a kitchen office can mean anything from providing a flat space for a message pad to building in a complete computer desk with keyboard shelf, monitor, CPU, and the requisite phone line for online connections. Either way, this dedicated area can provide the cook with a place to read cookbooks, plan shopping lists, pay bills, and take care of other household management tasks. It should be a step or more away from the actual food-prep areas to avoid dust, heat, and water around sensitive electronics and to help keep paperwork relatively grease and flour free (see the photo on the facing page). A standard-height desk chair and desk surface are also important both for ergonomics and to distinguish the desk area from preparation space. Standard desk height is 29 in. to 30 in., as opposed to counter surfaces at 36 in.

Putting the kitchen online is a natural step in the evolution of the kitchen as the central work area of the house. Dedicated computer multimedia systems with speakers, radio and cable tuners, and Internet access may be the norm by the time you read this. Some cookbooks are already online, and the day is near when grocery ordering and meal planning will be,

A blender may be a small appliance, but you still need to plan storage space for it and other appliances like it.

too. Wire your kitchen now for more than you think you'll ever need, and we have no doubt that you'll find yourself tapping into the online world sooner than you think.

Countertop Appliances

Any discussion of appliances and kitchen design would be incomplete without a mention of countertop, or portable, appliances. Not only do they require planning and space, but they also have a great deal to do with the overall function and style of the space. Many appliances represent the cutting edge of industrial design and stand out as interesting objects in their own right. They also represent a significant

expense when you add up all the toasters, mixers, pasta machines, bread machines, coffeemakers, and other small appliances found in the average kitchen.

Storage for a random assortment of small appliances can mean the difference between a comfortable kitchen and one where you're always moving things out of the way. Plan space for appliances based on how often you use them and on their weight, size, and function. A coffeemaker used every day may stay in its own dedicated spot on the counter near a seating area and sink. A heavy mixer may be pushed into an appliance garage when it's not being used. Hand appliances can be stored in deep drawers near areas where they'll be used. As you plan your work areas and cabinetry, consider developing an inventory of small appliances and devising a place for each.

All of these appliances and electronics offer you the opportunity to focus on details of look, material, and function. Choosing a group that works together on a functional level while looking good together is a challenge, albeit an interesting one. Consider the look of handles, knobs, and finishes, as well as the overall design aesthetic used by the appliance designer. A retro '50s stove would look out of place next to a stainless-steel commercial refrigerator. On the other hand, nothing says your appliances must all match each other. The important thing is to consider how they fit into the overall design when choosing any appliance.

CHAPTER 8

Cabinetry and Work Surfaces

I f you took everything out of your kitchen and piled it in another room, you'd have an interesting mound of things representing a variety of storage problems. Many of the things would be perishable, delicate, or odd shaped. Some would be heavy, and some would be very small. Looking at this variety of things would bring the realization that a kitchen must have efficient storage space to work well.

For many of us, our first consideration when planning a kitchen is cabinets. Cabinetry is the organizing factor in kitchen design. It provides space for storage and support for work surfaces. It provides places to sit, creates traffic patterns, and connects appliances. It houses all kinds of

The use of lazy Susans and swing-out cabinet inserts is not restricted to corner cabinets. Even straight-run lower cabinets have interior space that is difficult to access without inserts.

Pull-out shelves in lower cabinets make all usable space easily accessible from above.

Pull-down sink trays that mount behind cabinet panels offer a water-resistant storage place for sponges.

specialized space designed for storing the multitude of unusual tools found in every kitchen. The quality of its construction and materials determines how well it will function and for how long. It's surfaced with interesting materials that should enhance the overall style and atmosphere of the space.

Decisions about cabinetry are complex. There are dozens of sizes, shapes, specialized designs, door styles, drawer and drawer-front styles, and types of hardware. You'll find both natural and man-made materials, from particleboard to stainless steel. In this chapter, we're going to look at cabinetry and how to use it to make your kitchen look good and work well. We'll also look at the many work surfaces available. These work surfaces, when installed correctly, become an integral part of the cabinetry system. Because you'll use the surfaces daily, decisions regarding materials, location, and shape will have a significant effect on the function of your new kitchen.

The Evolution of the Box

The kitchen cabinets widely available today are basically boxes. They are stacked, screwed to walls, and arranged in rows. They are then covered with counters, doors, drawer fronts, and decorative panels. Some may contain special inserts for trays, recycling bins, pull-out shelves, and even ironing boards and cutting boards. These boxes form the core storage areas and support the work surfaces that make your kitchen function well. The key to planning your kitchen's cabinetry is to focus on these two functions.

The modular nature of cabinets is a fairly recent development. Early kitchen cabinetry was either free-standing furniture (unfitted) or built-in-place cabinets similar to those found in pantries (fitted). Kitchens often had few cabinets, due in part to the fact that shopping was done daily. Work surfaces were usually freestanding tables. In the '30s and '40s, most cabinets were built in place by carpenters who started with raw lumber and built cabinets on-site that were an integral part of the building, using the

These cabinets were built on-site by the carpenter who did the original trim in this 1920 home. They have face-frame construction with inset glass panel doors, and the wall acts as the back of the cabinet.

Above: *Euro-style cabinetry has a sleeker appearance than the more traditional face-frame cabinetry.*

Left: *Face-frame cabinets offer many visual options. In this example, the vertical frames are fluted and serve as a decorative element. This is also an example of inset doors.*

walls themselves as structural elements (see the photo on the facing page). The cabinets' quality was entirely dependent on the skill level of the carpenter who built them.

Anyone who has tried to remove these built-in cabinets knows that they don't come off in one piece because they are not boxes but rather frames nailed to walls and covered with doors. When factory-made cabinets began to appear in the '40s, they were boxes but they still had frames on the front to hang doors on. This style of cabinetry, known as face-frame cabinets (see the left photo above), was the dominant form of cabinetry, particularly in the United States, until the '80s when European, or Euro-style, cabinets began to appear.

EURO-STYLE CABINETS

Euro-style cabinetry came out of a peculiarly European tradition. In parts of Europe, cabinets were made to easily knock down so they could be removed from the house during a move, along with the furniture. Special knockdown fittings and hinges that allowed the use of doors without face frames made it easy to take your cabinets apart and stack them up for moving. It also made manufacturing very simple, especially with the advent of computer-controlled machinery and high-quality panel stock.

There are several advantages to Euro-style cabinets over traditional face frames. Face frames take up space and limit access to the interior of the cabinet. Euro-style cabinetry has a sleek appearance because all visible surfaces are covered by the door or drawer front (see the right photo above). A comparable-width face-frame lower cabinet will have much

Hinges used on Euro-style cabinets are invisible when the cabinet is closed, yet they provide a pivoting action that allows closely set doors to open without interference.

With Euro-style cabinets, you can get fuller access to the interior than you can get with face-frame cabinets.

smaller drawers than its Euro-style counterpart because the drawers must fit in between the frames. In a typical lower four-drawer cabinet, the difference is over 1 sq. ft. of lost space.

Euro-style cabinets are becoming much more prevalent in the United States as factories come on line with the computer numerically controlled (CNC) machinery required to make the many standard parts. The system has a great deal of flexibility for shelving, inserts, drawers, and other interior features because it has a universal system of holes, drawer slides, hinges, and other hardware. The hinges used have a double action that brings a door toward you to clear adjacent doors before it starts to swing; these hinges allow you to open doors up to 180 degrees (see the top photo at left). This makes more of the interior accessible, which is especially important on lower cabinets where there is often wasted space (see the bottom photo at left).

The cabinets you choose should be based on function and how they will integrate with your existing cabinetry. Combining Euro-style with face-frame cabinetry can result in an odd mix of styles, or it can work well, depending on the surfacing used. Even custom cabinetry made specifically for your kitchen will likely come from one of these two schools.

FREESTANDING CABINETS

The '80s saw a trend back toward the unfitted, or furniture-style, kitchen, particularly in Great Britain. Unfitted kitchen cabinets are individual pieces of furniture, often freestanding and usually with their own integrated tops. The resulting kitchens feature high levels of craftsmanship but often func-

tion poorly due to uneven work surfaces, unconnected runs of counter, and a trend-driven determination not to look new. Unfitted cabinetry can work well as islands or work tables that float in a room with a design presence of their own.

Cabinet Design Elements

The vertical surfaces of cabinets form an important design element in your new kitchen that you'll interact with on a daily basis. Decisions about style and materials should be based on both visual impact and practical use.

DOORS AND DRAWER FRONTS

The photos throughout this book show a wide range of door styles. Doors and drawer fronts can be inset or overlay, depending on their relationship to the front cabinet edge. Inset doors require careful fitting and quality construction because there is little room for adjustment. Overlay doors fit on top of the cabinet front and are usually equipped with adjustable hinges that allow the installer to align all the doors by turning a few screws. With face-frame cabinets, frames may be visible and can offer a material or color contrast to the doors. Euro-style boxes are completely covered by their doors except for a narrow gap, or reveal. These reveals provide an attractive visual line for the eye to follow.

Keep in mind when choosing material, finish, and door style that doors and drawer fronts are a major factor in the overall appearance of your kitchen. An expanse of overly complex doors or a radical color scheme can overwhelm the other design elements of the room. A simple clean design will serve as a neutral backdrop for food and the tools in the kitchen.

HARDWARE

Many new kitchens are near completion before the designers and owners start considering hardware. However, choosing visible items like door and drawer pulls is an important part of the overall design process because these elements are touched and noticed by every person who uses the kitchen (see the photos at right). Even a small kitchen may have 30 to 40 of these pulls, which means they represent both a considerable expense and a frequently recurring design element.

As with appliances, we recommend you explore the many hardware options available beyond those standard ones found in home centers. Choosing an elegant or high-concept set of pulls and other hardware can give even a basic kitchen some of the elegance found in higher-priced kitchens.

Hardware is not limited to visible elements. Better-quality hinges and drawer slides also make a noticeable improvement in the daily use of the kitchen. Quality drawer slides in particular are important because of the weight of objects typically stored in kitchen drawers. A lightweight drawer slide can break, jam, or cause heavily laden drawers to drop when fully extended. Don't let your kitchen-cabinet supplier skimp on these important items. The few dollars saved will mean many headaches later as the items start to fail.

Hardware like these door pulls is not only a practical part of your kitchen but also a design element.

Inventory Your Storage Needs

Remember that pile of stuff in the beginning of this chapter? While we're not really suggesting that you pile your kitchen items up somewhere and count them, we do recommend careful consideration of how much storage you need, what goes in storage, and where the storage will be located. An inventory of the items you commonly use and those that are rarely used can serve as a guide to planning your storage needs. Commonly used foods and utensils should be easily accessible, while that fondue pot you use once a decade should be banished to a back cupboard or sent to the local garage sale.

Plan your cabinetry needs based on the use and function of each area. Start with cabinets connecting the sink area with the refrigerator and range. These connections determine what functions and storage will be needed in those spaces. For instance, the area

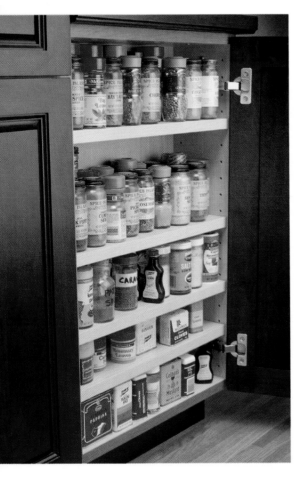

This narrow spice cabinet makes good use of a shallow area. Ideally, spices and herbs should be located near the stove because they are used most often during cooking.

Consider using divided drawers in areas where you need utensils close at hand. They also work well for linen storage.

between a sink and a stove may hold cutting boards, knives, pots and pans, and cooking utensils. The storage near the stove may hold herbs and spices that are added during cooking, oils and other condiments, and canned goods (see the top photo at left). Between the sink and the refrigerator is a food-storage and prep area for cold foods. Bowls, storage containers, mixers, colanders, and other food-prep items may be found here. By the same logic, cleaning supplies end up near the sink, and dish storage is near the dishwasher.

Work Surfaces

Work surfaces, or counters, come in standard sizes or can be fabricated to fit your design. The standard height used in U.S. kitchens is 36 in. Standard depth from front edge to backsplash is 24 in. These dimensions work well for a range of people, and unless you are designing a kitchen for persons with special requirements, you should stick with the standards as guidelines. Unusual variance from standard height may mean a kitchen that won't work for future owners. If you are designing for a person with special requirements, you'll need to adjust the ergonomics of the kitchen to fit that person's individual needs and restrictions.

Factory-made counters may work for short, straight runs, but there is no way to adjust for walls out of square, unusual shapes, or cut-outs to fit around trim or appliances. A custom counter is scribed to fit around all unusual dimensions by the builder, ensuring a tight, attractive fit. This becomes especially important when you consider the fact that water and dirt can easily find any open joints or cracks.

Above: *This baking area groups storage for baking staples, tools, and appliances and features its own sink and granite-counter insert.*

Right: *This detail of the baking area shows an upper cabinet designed to store bowls within easy reach of the work surface.*

Counters are horizontal surfaces, which means they receive much more wear and tear than vertical surfaces. People set heavy pans and dishes on them, use them as cutting surfaces, and generally beat them up over time. Because of this, it's important to consider your ability to have your counters replaced in the future when they become worn.

Work-surface materials vary from ceramic tile to laminate, stone, man-made solid surfaces, and wood. Each has its strengths and weaknesses. Ceramic-tile counters are very hard, and the grout lines between tiles can stain easily. Laminate counters offer a very wide range of finishes and color, and they are inexpensive and very flexible in installation. They are also susceptible to water damage, scratching, and burns, and they have a man-made patina that some may not care for. A granite counter lasts virtually forever, looks great, and is relatively immune to heat. However, it is very costly to make and install and offers a very hard nonresilient surface to deli-

Above: *While the main work surface in this kitchen is the standard height, specialized work areas and seating areas have their own functional heights.*

Right: *Inserting a section of a different counter material is a design option that can enhance the function and appearance of the kitchen. A marble pastry surface is perfect for baking preparation.*

Backsplashes protect walls from food stains and water damage. Decorative tiles like those below can be used to add color to a plain backsplash.

cate dishes and glassware. Counters made of wood stain and scratch, and some woods like cherry will darken or change appearance over time.

Your choice of materials is not limited to only one. It is common to insert a maple butcher block or marble pastry surface into a counter made of other materials (see the photos on the facing page). These inserts offer both a functional surface for specialized tasks and a delineation of those custom areas. They also provide design interest and variation.

Backsplashes

The walls behind work surfaces are particularly susceptible to splatters and water damage. They are often difficult areas to clean because of overhanging upper cabinetry. For these reasons, a durable backsplash is usually installed where the counter meets the wall (see the photos above). These backsplashes may be integral parts of the counters or a surface applied to the wall. Common materials are tile, laminate, and stainless steel. Backsplashes offer you another area for design and color, and

it is common to find decorative tile patterns wrapping around the perimeter of a kitchen in the backsplash.

Cabinetry and work surfaces become architectural elements after they're installed because they affect the spatial character of the kitchen. In the next chapter, we'll look at designing in three dimensions and working with these spatial considerations. Before you finalize your cabinet layout, you'll need to consider how it works with the overall architecture of the room.

CHAPTER 9

Architecture and Style

W e've been focusing on the basic spatial considerations involved in creating a kitchen that works, but we've yet to address architectural design or style. Before making style choices you need to become knowledgeable about how you use your kitchen and the existing space you have to work with, then you can make choices of colors, surfaces and materials, and the rest of the more visible elements of your kitchen.

The architectural heritage of your region, city, street, and individual house should have a significant impact on your overall design, even if you are determined to make a complete break with the trends that exist now. Even the most radical architectural break must still consider basic function, social use, and the climate. These considerations were often major determiners of what made your regional style what it is, and your new design will inevitably reflect them.

Architecture in kitchen design deals with the best use of three-dimensional space within the limitations of your budget and the room you have to work with. For our purposes, architectural elements are structural uses of space, historical reference in those uses, and the various built-in design features of your kitchen that reflect those uses. Style is made up of those visual elements that add color, texture, and ambience to the basic architectural shell of the room. To clarify this potentially confusing but important distinction, we need to take a look at style and architecture.

The Roots of Style

If architecture deals with how your building is designed and built, style deals with the look that makes it aesthetically pleasing to live and work in. Styles can be historical or driven by current trends. The Victorian style is a historical one based on the look of a specific time period. Restaurant-style kitchens are based on trends in appliance design, as well as on a desire to build a room that functions like its

commercial counterpart. Style can be a combination of history and trends, too. A good example might be a kitchen design that blends restaurant-style function with a historical style like English manor house. In this case, you might match commercial appliances with large work tables, surfacing materials like stone and ceramics, and large freestanding ceramic sinks. The result is a blend of old and new.

Recent architectural trends, such as postmodernism and deconstructionism, also serve as inspiration for style and are rapidly being assimilated into current kitchen design. Whether they will stand the test of time has yet to be seen. These cutting-edge approaches to design can be fun to plan and build,

but they run the considerable risk of becoming dated at an early age. Some trends may limit your choices and function. Designing an extremely minimalist kitchen, for instance, would mean creating unobtrusive storage that hides all unused items and choosing appliances based on a sleek, uninterrupted design aesthetic.

Styles often determine many of the surface and decoration decisions involved in creating a kitchen. These include: molding and trim; hardware; door and window styles; lighting styles; finishes and surfacing materials, including paint, counters, and floors; and cabinetry construction, panels, and drawer fronts (see the left photo on the facing page). An Arts and

A new kitchen in a Victorian-era home may not be Victorian in style, but its designer must still work with the common elements of this style, including tall windows and doors, high ceilings, and little uninterrupted wall space. (Illustration courtesy Dover Publications.)

FRONT ELEVATION.

Above: *To provide a continuity of styles, the molding detail on the cabinet was designed to match the existing door.*

Right: *This transition between the kitchen and dining area is successful because the cabinetry is stepped back to a shallower depth near the door, creating a wider passageway while still offering a perfect place for a coffeemaker just out of sight of the more formal dining area.*

Crafts-style kitchen, for example, will exhibit its style in all of these areas. Based on architectural trends late in the nineteenth century, the Arts and Crafts movement stressed plain, functional design and the use of native materials and hand-craftsmanship. So an Arts and Crafts kitchen might use fumed white oak cabinetry and moldings, warm earth-tone colors, handmade hanging lamps of glass and copper, hammered copper hardware, and Art Nouveau rugs. All of these things are representative design elements of the Arts and Crafts style that serve as a useful guide in making decisions.

Region and History

The location and age of your home will have a major impact on many of your design decisions. This does not necessarily mean you cannot put a contemporary kitchen in a Victorian home. It does mean that you must work with the high ceilings, large windows, elaborate trim, and multitude of doorways often found in these homes. All of these elements can be viewed as obstacles or benefits, depending on your willingness to work with or against the architecture.

There is a strong trend to go back to the historical roots of the home for guidance in planning a new kitchen. In its best use, this trend means incorporating the best developments in modern design, like improved appliances and materials, with the most interesting historical elements of the house. Thus, we might find a '50s ranch house with a very new kitchen that marries the latest Euro cooktop to a counter made of laminate festooned with an updated version of the boomerang pattern popular when the home was built. Modern functional elements linked with the heritage of the house can still result in an attractive space and enhanced usability.

The region you live in also determines architectural style. Geographic location has a strong effect on how your home is built. Typically homes are built of local materials from nearby resources. One town may feature a preponderance of brick homes because of a nearby source of clay for brick

making. Travel 100 miles, and you may find that most of the houses are wood frame because of the forests that covered the nearby terrain when the town was founded. Other regional building styles based on indigenous materials include southwestern adobe construction and the Spanish-style stucco homes of Southern California.

Interior material choices may also be dictated by regional materials. Natural wood trim and molding, flooring, and cabinets may be chosen because of the area you reside in. The use of northeastern hardwoods like maple and white oak and southern woods like cypress contribute to the regional design and style of your house.

Today we have international sources of building materials with

choices coming from every corner of the planet. Nothing says you must respect historical or regional conventions in your design. However, these patterns can serve as an excellent starting point in the many decisions involved in creating your kitchen.

Location also determines many structural decisions (see the right photo on p. 111). Expansive views may call for walls of windows while an unpleasant view may be minimized by utilizing skylights to bring in light and air from above. Carefully placed windows can frame a desirable view of a small garden, for instance, while excluding a nearby parking lot or alley. Location is not merely a visual consideration; locations often mean dealing with noise, privacy, air pollution, and other environmental problems. Architecturally this may mean placing a public room between a noisy street and a quiet room, such as a bedroom or study. In that case, your kitchen may serve as a buffer between that noisy street and a good night's sleep.

Climate is also a major architectural influence. New England saltbox homes had low ceilings to reduce the volume of space that needed heating. The long winters also required a multitude of fireplaces and chimneys and large steep roofs designed to shed heavy snow loads. Head south to Florida and

In this remodel, the integration of old and new was poorly handled. A better solution would have been to remove the old lower cabinets, which have limited appeal, and to build a new cabinet that fits smoothly with the new counter. The attractive glass-fronted upper cabinets would remain and serve as a model for new upper cabinetry elsewhere in the kitchen.

the emphasis is on cooling, with large windows, wide exterior overhangs for shade, screened porches, and open, unplastered frame walls painted in light, bright colors. Even with modern climate-control systems and improved energy efficiency, these climate-driven choices should be respected.

Integrating Existing Elements

In a remodeled kitchen, you may have the option of incorporating existing architectural elements within the design of your new kitchen. Interesting moldings like chair rails, crown moldings, and various detailing can visually connect your new kitchen with the older house. Existing built-in-place cabinetry, often found in pantries and old kitchens, may be saved or may serve as a design guide for new cabinetry. Often your new kitchen can be an upgrade of the old combined with best features available in new elements.

Integrating existing moldings and other architectural elements can be accomplished by matching new pieces to old (see the left photo on p. 111). For instance, your carpenter can have new crown molding made that matches the profile of existing moldings. Even if these new moldings are smaller or have a different finish, they could be used to trim out cabinets while maintaining the feel of the older room. Other simple ways to integrate old and new include using the same materials, colors, and hardware as the original on the new additions or cabinetry.

Much of the character of an older home is found in architectural elements like the trim shown in the room above and surrounding the Arts and Crafts-style stained glass window at right. Good design seeks to integrate older elements with newer ones to maintain the historical feel of the room or house.

Just keep lifestyle in mind when you make these style choices. It's important to consider how these architectural influences will affect your lifestyle and to make choices accordingly, rather than simply following a trend you loved in a magazine, book, or friend's home. The most alluring kitchens you see may work extremely well for their owners but may not be suited to the way you live.

CHAPTER 10

Designing with Color and Texture

Creating a kitchen that not only works well but also lives well involves much more than choosing the right appliances or filling the room with custom cabinetry. While these practical considerations are vital to the success of your kitchen design, they are only a part of the overall ambience that defines a comfortable, livable kitchen. Color, texture, the flow of light across a room, the mix of materials and finishes, and the three-dimensional character of the kitchen must all work in concert.

The challenge of choosing and coordinating these visual and tactile elements can be a difficult one. Even the most serene and minimal of modern designs require a very careful balance of color, light, and detail. The range of the color gray, for instance, extends from a warm off-white to a cool slate-blue, with every shade imaginable in between. While all these shades may be grays, the final effect of each may be very different. Combine that effect with a choice of related textures, colors, and materials, and achieving that minimalist design becomes a real challenge.

Color is more than a tone on a paint chip or a dyed thread in a fabric swatch. It is the way that paint tone looks splashed across a wall with a range of daylight crossing it. It is influenced by other colors reflected off of nearby objects or surfaces. It is combined with the texture of the surface it is on, a texture that reflects light in its own unique way. These influences can make that color seem cooler or warmer, darker or lighter, brighter or more muted.

Your kitchen design should take into consideration all of these influences, the many materials involved, and the overall result. To consider all of these things, you need to develop a palette of color, texture, and, ultimately, materials to work from while creating your design. To develop such a palette, you can use one of several different processes, or models. In this chapter, we'll look at two: reference models and historical models.

This turned bowl with its caramel-colored rim served as inspiration for the color-texture palette of its owner's new kitchen shown at right.

Reference Models

Choosing the right color and texture palette for your kitchen means making many choices while remaining flexible and trying to keep an overall look in mind. This ability to visualize a finished room from a handful of fabric swatches, paint chips, and material samples is an acquired skill. It helps to have a model for making these difficult choices, a model that gives you a reference point for the overall look you want.

A reference model is a group of objects, a photo, artwork, or some other visual example you find appealing. This source serves as a point of reference for choosing colors and textures

for your kitchen design (see the photos above and on the facing page). It's important to consider this reference model an inspiration rather than a hard-and-fast guide. It might be possible to literally duplicate the colors in a photo and then carefully find materials that are exact matches. The results would probably not match your expectations. Instead, try using your reference model as a starting point. The

The birch cabinetry and deep purple and brown granite counter were derived in spirit from the turned birch bowl in the photo above, setting the tone for the overall color and texture of this kitchen.

purpose of exercises like these is to learn to visualize on an abstract level and then apply that vision to your practical design problems. The final result should be an aesthetically pleasing and functional kitchen.

Developing a reference model and creating a palette based on it will take experimentation. Inspiration will be found in unexpected places. For example, you need not rely on paint chips for color choices. Any object with a color you like can be taken to a reputable paint dealer and matched to derive a paint color. The same goes for choices about everything from laminate to hardware. When matching, it's not necessary to find perfection; instead, seek the same tone and range as the color you've chosen and try your material sample against your original source for compatibility.

The nice thing about this approach is that one color or texture can lead you to others, often resulting in an unexpected juxtaposition that works. Occasionally, the model will contain a vivid color like the intense green in the grape arbor photo on the facing page. Experienced designers seek these more radical elements and insert them carefully into a design with restraint. Sometimes a luxuriant material color or an exotic detail can lift the whole design scheme to another level.

In assembling your palette, don't forget to try a range of materials. Stone next to steel next to laminate next to paint is something that will occur many places in your finished kitchen. Once you start finding a basic set of three or four colors and textures to work with, get actual samples of materials and paint chips and try them together in the room under varying lighting conditions. Don't scrimp here. If you're unsure about a color or texture, buy a few square feet of tile or a finished wood door and look at it on a larger scale. A few extra dollars spent on experimentation can mean less money spent trying to get it right after the fact.

Let's look at two such reference models, one based on a photograph and the other on a grouping of favorite objects. These models will show you how to choose a basic group of colors and textures and how to work from this group to pick materials based on their relationship to your model.

GRAPE ARBOR PHOTO

Our first example is based on a photo of a grape arbor in early fall. For the kitchen, we chose colors from the photo that naturally work together, and we also used it as a reference for textural and architectural cues like the bark on the old vines and the molding details on the arbor. These elements were then used to assemble several groups of potential materials for the final kitchen. Finally, these choices became the basis for the actual finished look of the kitchen.

This photo is the reference model for our first example. Its intense lighting, color balance, and range of textures make it an appealing starting point for assembling an unusual color and texture palette.

The design process begins by choosing elements of the photo that have a distinctive color and/or textural quality. In this case, we chose the deep green and reddish browns of the leaves and vines, the purple of the grapes, and the gray color of the trellis.

We started by selecting several areas of the photo that showed colors or textures that we liked. The bright green and rust-brown of the leaves, the weathered creamy gray paint, and the purple of the grapes themselves were good starting points (see the photos above). We knew they worked together well in the photo; the challenge was to translate this harmony into the choices we needed to make for our kitchen design.

After making these color and texture choices from the model, we had a guide for choosing material samples. The next step was to take each color or texture range and assemble samples of the various kitchen materials that fit in that range. Each of the photos (see the facing page and p. 122) shows a group of tile, wood, laminate, and other typical kitchen materials that share a similar tone and texture. These samples can be obtained at any commercial supplier of each material, at your local home centers, or through designers. As you search for your samples, you'll begin to understand why a model like this can be so valuable. There are so many choices that it helps to find some method of narrowing down your range. In this example, the elements in the photo provided that model.

Choices should not be based only on color. Consider sheen, texture, resiliency (the way the material responds to touch), and other elements, like the transparency of the finish. Try not to limit yourself at this stage by

Top: *Using the purple of the grapes as a reference, we assembled a group of samples with the same color range. At this point we weren't looking for specific materials, just possible choices for later.*

Bottom: *The vibrant green of the leaves is reflected in these materials.*

price or any prejudice regarding various materials. Just gather your samples by tonal and textural range. Once you've assembled them, you can start to group the different elements to try various combinations.

Our final choices began with the selection of a bright green Mexican tile (see the top left photo on the facing page). Its glossy sheen and reflective qualities were eye-catching, and we knew that if we decided to use it, the other materials would have to work in harmony with it rather than in competition. The purple of the grapes required care because matching two strong colors like purple and green can be a challenge. We found a laminate sample that had the color but also had a fine sandy texture in it that muted the purple nicely.

Taking a cue from the reddish brown of the leaves, we decided to use oak upper cabinet doors stained a mahogany-brown, with the contrasting grain highlighted by the stain (see the bottom photo on the facing page). The gloss of the finish carried over from the green tile. We knew the lower cabinetry would have to be more subdued to counterbalance the strong color palette outlined above. A grayish beige color chosen from a historical paint chart matched the color of the old trellis, and a simple molding around the panels echoed its architectural lines (see the top right photo on the facing page). Finally, our choice of clear glass panels in the upper cabinets and brushed bronze hardware for all

These material choices were influenced by the rust-red of the early fall leaves in the grape arbor photo on p. 119.

Above left: *Inspired by the grape arbor photo, this intense green handmade tile works well with the purple laminate counter.* Above right: *The lower cabinets are painted a historical gray/beige inspired by the trellis color.* Left: *The reddish brown stain and open grain of these upper cabinet doors was based on the reddish brown of the leaves and vines. The glass inserts reflect light, while the bronze pulls also carry the fall color theme.*

of the cabinets helped convey some of the intense lighting that made the photo so attractive.

The result is an unconventional look that combines the intensity of the green and purple with the elegance of traditional cabinetry (see the photo at left), a combination we would have been unlikely to consider without the influence of the photo.

FAVORITE OBJECTS

In our second example, the color palette began with a few favorite objects chosen for their muted colors and textural interest. The original idea was to create a somewhat restrained design that would serve as a backdrop for the bright colors of cooking tools and food. We assembled a still life from various objects, some from around the house and others gathered during walks on the beach. The final selection combines a black-iron Japanese teapot, pieces of driftwood, and the muted hues of old shells (see the photo on the facing page).

We assembled our material samples based on the black, coal-colored, and dark metallic textures of the driftwood and iron teapot; on the creamy whites and reddish browns of the shells; and on the weathered quality of the lighter piece of driftwood (see the photos on pp. 126-128). As in the previous example, we assembled kitchen-material samples that matched the colors and textures in our group of objects.

The final look is an unexpectedly harmonious mixture of bright color and elegant styling. The balance of the original photo has been successfully carried into the overall design and material choices.

This grouping of objects was chosen for its muted yet interesting mixture of color and texture. The shells, driftwood, and black-iron teapot were chosen for both their inherent color and texture and the way they look together.

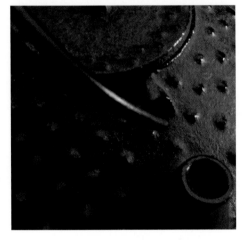

The color and texture of the dark driftwood (top) and this Japanese black-iron teapot (above) were the influences behind the material choices shown at right.

These material choices were influenced by the lighter driftwood.

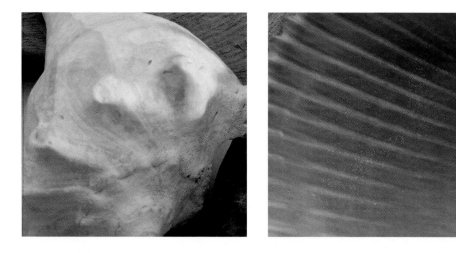

The shells (left) served as a reference point in choosing the materials shown below.

Again, an unusual tile, this time a natural stone material, set the tone for the overall design. These tiles are made of tumbled marble, a material that closely mimics the look of the worn stone pavers you'd find in a Mediterranean village (see the top photo at right). Complex in texture and carrying a surprisingly wide range of tones, they reflect several appealing elements of both shells. These elements include the sea-worn patina, the rust and cream colors, and the softly rounded texture you feel when you handle a shell.

The palette of blacks presented an interesting challenge. The iron Japanese teapot was highly textural with a slightly glossy feel, while the black driftwood was grainy. Our materials palette contained hand-wrought iron hardware, black granite, laminates, and dark-dyed woods. Our final choices were small but very tactile handmade iron pulls and a man-made solid surfacing material for the counter that had a grainy look but was very smooth (see the left bottom photo at right), offering an interesting contrast to the rough marble tile.

While we liked the wood grain of the brown driftwood in the original grouping, we eventually varied from the formula and chose a washed gray finish over beadboard panel doors (see the bottom right photo at right). The grain of the wood shows through, and the beadboard is a reminder of cottages near the water. The slightly weather-beaten look of the finish also echoed the weather-beaten textures of the driftwood.

These tumbled marble tiles have a shell-like pitted texture and the range of color found in both shells in the original grouping. They serve as a strong element binding the more muted materials into a coherent design.

The black-iron knob and smooth counter material were chosen based on the feel of the iron teapot and the darker driftwood in the original grouping.

The final finish on the cabinets was chosen for its muted, weather-beaten look. While the gray is not an exact match to the driftwood in the reference model, it still carries the overall tone of the group.

The result is a restrained but visually interesting kitchen that has a wide range of textural elements (see the photo at left). The tumbled marble is a material that conveys a feeling of history and permanence, while the thoroughly modern counter material reminds us that this is a space dedicated to practical pursuits. The muted, almost monochromatic range of color is broken by the rusty reds in the tile and would serve admirably as a backdrop for entertaining and cooking.

Historical Models

Another common model for developing a palette of colors and textures is the historical model. If you wish to base your kitchen design on an historical precedent or a school of design, much of the basic palette for that model already exists. Research into the thought behind that school or period's style, the defining reasons behind those thoughts, and research into other kitchens using that style will give you a range of choices. For example, the Shakers were a utopian society that revered simplicity and craftsmanship and maintained an extremely austere lifestyle that stressed work and spirituality. They were consummate designers and woodworkers who used materials available on their own land. Colors were based on those easily derived from natural sources.

Researching these cultural reasons for the beauty of the Shaker style provides you with a set of guidelines for your color and texture decisions

This is the completed look that began with the inspiration of the collection of shells, driftwood, and the teapot.

Shaker style is based on the combination of two ideals—simplicity and purity—and the use of locally available materials. (Photo ©Brian Vanden Brink.)

should you choose to build a Shaker-influenced kitchen. It does not mean that you must create a historical re-production, but it does mean you should keep in mind the restraints and underlying cultural influences that made that style so attractive (see the photo above). Simple Shaker cabinets feature plain panel doors, hand-cut joinery, and native northern hard-woods like cherry and maple. Building these cabinets with an exotic wood like mahogany would result in a dis-

tinctly non-Shaker aesthetic, as would using gold-plated hardware or some other equally sumptuous material. Simplicity in this example comes from a very disciplined paring away of nonessential elements.

The Shaker palette also provides a range of color choices based on the simple milk-based paints they had available and suggests materials like native soapstone or slate for sinks, counters, and other work surfaces. Because this range of choice is driven

This Pennsylvania colonial's kitchen and dining area reflect their historical model through the period lighting, low-beamed ceilings, and wide-plank floors. (Photo by Steve Culpepper.)

by a proven historical precedent, the colors and materials work well together and ideally should result in the same feeling of simple purity in look and function.

Colonial kitchens represent another historical precedent with many features unique to their period, including low ceilings, small windows, wide-plank floors, and a cozy atmosphere. The key is to integrate good lighting, to keep the space from feeling too closed in, and to support modern cooking equipment without changing the Early American ambience (see the photo above).

Design Challenges

The key to good visual and tactile design is balance. Hard and soft, bright and muted, angular and round are all examples of balancing elements. A minimal approach may call for at least one design-oriented object or artwork to focus one's attention on. A very busy design (like a Victorian kitchen) may be balanced by a view outdoors into a simple garden or an austere landscape. Finding the right combination of elements and blending them into a cohesive whole is a primary design challenge. Your kitchen will serve as a backdrop for working and socializing and as a comfortable space for living. Your design should also consider the practical application of the materials you choose. These additional design challenges should be considered when making choices in color, texture, and materials.

BACKDROP THINKING

Remember that your kitchen is the background for many brightly colored and textural things, including vegetables, flowers, dishes, pans, and other smaller objects. Exercising restraint with the overall design will allow these striking natural and man-made objects to stand out against the backdrop. Some colors may clash with food, resulting in unappetizing or harsh combinations that prove wearying over time. With a restrained palette featuring only one or two bright elements, you can always use art or flowers to bring out colors.

COMFORT LEVEL

The colors and textures you choose have an inherent comfort level. Extremely saturated or high-contrast colors can result in visual fatigue over time. Very bright reflective surfaces near sources of natural light can mean harsh glare on sunny days. Dark surfaces with inadequate, poorly targeted task lighting can mean eye strain. Tile or stone floors are fatiguing to stand on for long periods, and an abundance of stone and metal can contribute to a high noise factor.

These problems are design challenges that can often be countered by using their opposites. Muted wall colors can balance brightly colored elements (see the photo above). Reflections can be controlled with blinds. Good lighting masks a multitude of

The brightness of this kitchen's purple chairs is muted by the soft colors of the walls and cabinets. (Photo by Charles Miller.)

sins, especially if you provide a wide range of choices. Natural-fiber or rubber floor mats or throw rugs at busy areas relieve fatigue, and a carpeted area or upholstered furnishings will absorb sound.

PRACTICAL DESIGN CONSIDERATIONS

Certain colors and textures represent very practical problems. We've had problems with black-glazed ceramic sinks because every water mark and scratch shows up over time. Many porous stone and unglazed tile surfaces absorb oils, resulting in unsightly stains that are permanent. Sharp corners and hard surfaces can be safety

issues, especially where small children are present. Using painted walls in lieu of a backsplash for a minimalist look will mean frequent repainting as it is next to impossible to clean some food splatters off the water-based paints in use today.

Problem-solving in the design stage is an interesting process based on finding solutions that counteract and balance each other. Problem-solving after construction is underway is expensive and frustrating as you start redoing costly work or designing by trial and error. Develop a color and texture palette as a guide and then use balance and restraint to resolve problems before you begin to build.

CHAPTER 11

The Material World

In no other room do so many materials converge, and nowhere else are they subjected to the same extremes of abuse as in the kitchen. The wide range of materials, both man-made and natural, found in even the most basic kitchen means that you must make numerous decisions about those materials every step of the way. These decisions affect your budget, your construction schedule, the look of your kitchen, and how well it works for years to come.

In this chapter, we're going to look at surface and flooring materials that you can choose for your kitchen from both an aesthetic and a practical viewpoint. Construction materials used under these visible surfaces are not covered except as they affect your choice in a given material. These construction considerations are covered in detail in Part 3.

As we noted in the last chapter, both design challenges and practical considerations must be addressed with each material choice. Some materials that look great are not durable enough for kitchen use, while other eminently practical materials may not enhance your design. Combine these considerations with your attempts to create a coherent overall design, and your knowledge of the material world becomes an important part of the design learning process.

Materials Palette

As part of your research, you should begin assembling a materials palette to help you coordinate the color, texture, feel, and function of the many surfaces in your kitchen. This palette may consist of wood and stone samples; manufacturers' samples of laminates, tile, and various man-made materials; and samples you've collected for matching to a color or texture that you find appealing.

Like the range of choices in cabinetry or appliances, the materials that make up your kitchen have many properties. They not only have color and texture, but they are also tactile, meaning they're either resilient or hard, warm or cold. Various materials reflect light differently, react to water and foods differently, require specialized construction or underlayments, and may be finished different ways.

Like the color and texture palette we looked at in Chapter 10, a materials palette helps you make the many decisions involved in choosing what your kitchen will be made of. These decisions are not only aesthetic, but they are also practical, requiring some knowledge of how various materials will wear over time. Building a materi-

Wood is used for everything from floors to cabinetry to trim, depending on the type of wood.

als palette can help you create a kitchen that is both highly functional and attractive.

Wood

As a natural material, wood offers endless variation. There are hardwoods like maple and oak and softwoods like pine and cedar. There are blond woods like ash and dark woods like walnut. Grain patterns and textures vary widely, determined not only by species but also by how quickly the wood grew and how it was cut at the mill. Various woods react very differently to the effects of exposure to water or light. Oak may blacken when exposed to ammonia solutions, and maple naturally yellows over time when exposed to sunlight. All of these properties are important considerations when working with wood in a kitchen.

The finish is as important to the look of the wood as the species. Most factory and custom cabinetry come with a multicoat sprayed lacquer finish that should hold up well, especially on vertical surfaces. Floors receive thicker, harder finishes. Certain finishes may accentuate the grain of the wood. Or you can use dyes and stains to create wood finishes that can be virtually any color or shade imaginable while they still retain the wood's grain and character (see the photos at right and on p. 138).

At the core of many wood cabinets and counters are engineered wood products like medium-density fiberboard (MDF), a manufactured material that is very stable and can be cut easily and accurately. Engineered woods are very valuable in an abusive

In addition to choosing the type of wood, you will also have to choose a finish. Finishes not only protect, but they also can add color, enhance or mute grain patterns, and change the sheen or texture.

This washed green finish shows how wood can be enhanced with a colored finish.

Some old finishes develop a patina that adds to the wood's character.

environment like a kitchen because of their stability and durability. As a substrate for veneers or laminates, they are the preferred choice over solid wood, which is prone to warping, expansion, and contraction.

COUNTERS

Wood can be used for many things, including counters, floors, and cabinetry. In general, we think that wood counters only work if you are willing to accept the normal wear-marking that will accumulate over time. Maple butcher blocks are a popular choice, in part because maple is a very sanitary, hard, close-grained wood that holds up well to water. The downside is that it will yellow, stain, and scratch and may require periodic bleaching if you use it as a cutting surface. All finishes used on wood counters will scratch and wear. If you want a pristine, durable counter surface, consider another material and use a butcher block for a cutting or prep area. A butcher block is best left unfinished because most wood finishes will not hold up well on horizontal work surfaces.

FLOORS

Floors take a lot of abuse and require constant cleaning in kitchens. Softwoods like pine make very attractive floors but are susceptible to serious damage from heavy objects and things like high heels and metal chair legs, which can leave marks or holes. The finish on softwood flooring will wear quickly, requiring regular upkeep.

Hardwood floors are very durable and solid underfoot and are slightly more resilient than stone or tile. Traditionally, maple has been used for kitchen floors because of its natural resistance to water and its extreme hardness. Other woods may stain under repeated cleaning and spills.

New-technology hardwood floors combine a thin but durable wood veneer with a stable plywood base and are very easy to install and care for. They come in strips that fit together with a tongue-and-groove joint that is installed directly over a subfloor. Prefinished and easy to work, they do not require unusual construction or reinforcing, making it an easy way to resurface old floors with wood.

CABINETRY

Wood is the traditional material for cabinetry. It functions well, is very attractive, and offers a wide variety of practical choices. It's important when choosing a wood to consider the effect of a large expanse of wood doors and drawer fronts. You may find that a sample door made of walnut that looked great in a showroom overwhelms a room when its dark texture and color are spread over a large number of square feet. Popular woods include lighter species like maple and ash and more richly colored woods like cherry, which naturally darkens to a deep brown over time. Properly finished, almost any wood will work well for cabinet surfaces.

Ceramic Tile

Ceramic tile appears in kitchens as flooring, counters, and wall surfaces. Tile requires an extremely rigid and strong substrate, usually cement or a special backer board made of concrete material. Without this rigid backing, tile and its grout can crack, and tile repairs are very difficult to match with existing work.

The advantages of tile are beauty, color and sheen, heat and water resistance, and the tactile quality of its hard, smooth surface. It lends itself well to vertical applications like backsplashes and walls (see the photo below). We don't care for tile counters because dirt and oil can stain grout lines, water can cause damage, and the tile surface is very hard and can crack if heavy pans are dropped on it. If you choose tile as a counter surface, have the tile installed by a professional and choose tile made for horizontal applications.

Above: *Ceramic tile is available in styles ranging from historical to contemporary, with infinite variation in shape, glazing, texture, and size.*

Left: *Tile is well suited to vertical applications such as this backsplash, which features small, square tile with accents in green.*

This massive granite work surface is a strong design element that unites the many other materials used in this kitchen.

fired properly. Color in cheap tile may vary widely from samples and from box to box.

Floor tiles must be of high quality, made for flooring, and installed on a specially prepared concrete or multi-layer base. Any movement after installation will result in cracking. We don't recommend the use of unglazed tiles anywhere in a kitchen. They stain easily and cannot be cleaned thoroughly. Quality tiles have thick glazes that are fired at high temperatures by artisans who know how to create a durable product that is stable in dimension and color, which are both important in flooring.

The texture of tile varies from glossy to sandlike or stonelike. These rougher textures not only hold up well, but they also reduce slipperiness underfoot. Tiles also come in every look from a primitive paver to Victorian accent tiles to high-tech grids of color. A visit to several tile dealers will whet your appetite for this attractive and versatile material.

Stone

Stone has been used in kitchens since the beginning of time, appearing on floors, work surfaces, and even as a material for sinks and wood or coal-fired stoves. It is durable and has a timeless, natural look that will hold up virtually forever. Popular types of stone used in kitchens include marble for floors and counters, particularly in baking areas where it offers a cool surface for dough handling, granite for work surfaces (see the photo at left), and soapstone for sinks and counters. Stone flooring also may be made of slate or quarried regional stone pavers.

Tile ranges in price from very inexpensive, mass-produced squares to extremely expensive handmade, one-of-a-kind pieces. Cheap tile may work on a low-impact area like a backsplash, but it scratches easier than more expensive tile, is less dimensionally accurate, which yields an uneven installation, and can break if it's not

Stone is an expensive material usually found in higher-priced kitchens. Its use requires special construction because of its weight and its tendency to crack when exposed to horizontal loads. Fabricating stone counters and sinks is a specialized skill requiring stonecutting and polishing tools. Handling stone means maneuvering very heavy objects into place and making sure that all measurements are accurate, as cutting and trimming on-site may not be possible.

Like all natural materials, stone varies widely in color, texture, grain, and hardness. Granite makes an excellent counter material because it is not porous, takes a high polish, and comes in many colors and textures. Softer stone like slate and soapstone can stain or crack and may require some type of protective finish.

Choosing stone materials means seriously considering the long-term consequences of their use. Although expensive, they will remain functional for many lifetimes, even acquiring an attractive patina with time that cannot be duplicated. Porous stone like marble stains easily, and it may be impossible to remove some stains.

If you're on a limited budget but want the look or function of stone, consider using a section of granite or marble in one work area, preferably a baking area. Its cool, hard surface and unmatched appearance can give even a basic kitchen a professional look.

Metal

Kitchens are full of metal both as a surface material and in cookware. Common metals and finishes include stainless steel, enameled steel, cast iron, cast-copper and brass hardware,

Metal shows up in kitchens as hardware, as appliance surfaces, in metal-faced laminates, and in switch plates. It also is an important design element because of its widespread use in kitchen tools.

and anodized aluminum (see the photo above). Anodized metals have a durable, transparent, colored stain finish. You'll find metal on appliances, as hardware, as cabinet material, on counters, and in all kinds of other places. Things like stainless-steel or brass switch plates, pot racks, and fire screens all contribute to metal as a design element in your kitchen.

This large stainless-steel range hood is not only functional but also has a sculptural quality that adds to the ambience of this kitchen.

Consider coordinating the metals in your kitchen to create a unified look. A finish like brushed stainless steel can pull together varying elements like door pulls, appliances, switch plates, and pots and pans. Metal often shows up as a detail element in many areas, and having a unified style for these disparate elements can bring an entire design together.

Stainless steel is the material of choice in commercial appliances, cabinetry, and counter surfaces (see the photo above). It is steel with nickel and chromium added to produce a shiny, nonrusting, nontarnishing metal that is extremely durable and easy to care for. It is also expensive, and if you are considering custom installations, fabrication will add to the high cost. Factory-made stainless-steel cabi-

netry, work tables, and counters are available through commercial kitchen-supply dealers if you want the restaurant look and function they offer.

Stainless steel can be a cold material, and an abundance of stainless-steel cabinetry may result in a clinical-looking environment. Adding in textural elements and natural materials like a wooden butcher block and tile can warm up its polish. It is also reflective, meaning that a kitchen featuring a lot of stainless steel will be bright with reflected light.

Copper, brass, and cast iron also show up frequently in kitchens. They don't lend themselves to as many applications as stainless steel because they can oxidize or rust. In the case of copper and brass, this oxidation may result in an attractive green patina over time if left unpolished. These ma-

terials add a reflective warmth to any kitchen with their color and interesting texture. Copper is also an excellent conductor of heat, making it a sought-after material for cookware.

Synthetic Materials

Synthetic, or man-made, materials have been used in kitchens since the '40s when linoleum floors became popular. Until recently, man-made materials were perceived as relatively cheap substitutions for expensive natural materials. Now, with the advent of highly functional and attractive new man-made materials, they have become an important design element used for their own distinctive look (see the photo on the facing page).

Synthetic materials are found everywhere in the kitchen, but a primary use is in solid-surface and laminate work surfaces.

LAMINATES

Laminates are man-made surfacing materials made of paper and resins glued together at very high pressure. The resulting material is a thin, flat material that is hard, waterproof, and available in literally thousands of colors and textures. It is glued to a substrate, usually MDF or particleboard, and can be worked in many shapes. Laminate is an excellent choice for work surfaces because of its durability, cost-effectiveness, and the range of choice it offers. One concern can be the fabrication of the substrate and the quality of the workmanship. Poorly constructed counters or joints that are exposed to water can result in delamination and the destruction of the counter. Your best bet is to buy from a reputable fabricator who specializes in laminate work.

Laminate is also used for cabinetry, both on the interior surfaces and as a door surface. Laminate is easy to clean and will hold up well if it's made correctly. Quality construction is vital on edges, curved surfaces, and any place that comes in contact with water.

Recent innovations in laminate design and technology are making it

Solid surfacing materials make high-quality seamless counters when properly fabricated.

cleaned or sanded off, and you can get integral sinks that appear to be one molded piece with the surface around them.

These solid surfacing materials must be fabricated by factory-trained contractors who specialize in their use. When installed by authorized installers, they usually come with a long-term warranty against breakage and damage. The range of color and texture available has been greatly expanded in recent years, and the materials offer a very durable and attractive alternative to stone.

FLOORS

Synthetic flooring has been manufactured for many years, going back to the old patterned linoleum floors of the '40s. If you are removing these old floors or working in a house with them, bear in mind that many of them contain asbestos and should only be removed or covered by trained abatement workers.

Today, we have many choices in vinyl and composite floor tiles and sheet goods. Composite tiles with the color molded all the way through are a good inexpensive floor material. When you buy, specify commercial-grade tile, which will hold up well. Sheet vinyl ranges in quality from cheap material with the pattern printed on a thin top layer to quality products that are thicker and have the pattern molded through. Installation of sheet-vinyl products performed by experienced installers is worth the relatively small fees. You'll get a flat, pattern-matched floor with nearly invisible seams, which can be very difficult to accomplish without experience and specialized tools.

possible to use metallic surfaces in your kitchen without the expense of formed metal. Marrying the flexibility and cost-effectiveness of laminates with a thin veneer of metal, these metal laminates are available in a wide variety of finishes, patinas, metals, and textures. They are worked exactly the same as standard laminates, making their use accessible to most price ranges and design styles. Ask for samples from your laminate supplier.

SOLID SURFACING MATERIALS

There are many man-made substitutes for stone counters. Known generically as solid surfacing materials, they are found under brand names like Corian, and they are very expensive. Worked like solid wood with routers, saws, and drills and assembled with special glues, these materials offer a seamless, hard, solid surface that resembles granite (see the photo above). Stains can be

Glass

Glass doors give a kitchen an added source of light and provide display options. Glass is available in many finishes, including modern clear safety glass, sandblasted finishes, molded finishes like ripples and other patterns, antique glass with its charming imperfections, and many other choices (see the photo above). Mirrored glass can be used to expand a space visually or to bring light around corners. Glass is also used for backsplashes and wall coverings, providing an easy-to-clean, interesting surface on these vertical applications.

The many finishes available mean that using glass in doors does not necessarily mean displaying the contents

Fabric

Nothing adds natural texture and a range of color like the judicious use of fabrics in a kitchen. We say judicious because fabrics are not practical near work areas, particularly around open flames or smoky cooking. However, they do work well as upholstery in a sit-down area, as translucent window coverings, and as area rugs. These uses of fabrics give you the opportunity to inject color and to soften the often hard-edged design of most kitchens. You can use the colors in a favorite fabric as a guide in choosing an overall color scheme by "pulling out" certain colors and using them for paint and other color choices.

Fabric for kitchens must be durable and easily cleaned. Most upholstery materials are available with stain-repellent finishes, which are a necessity where people eat and drink. Look for fabrics with the pattern and color woven in rather than printed on the surface. They are more durable, attractive on both sides when used as curtains, and will retain their appearance much longer. We'll talk more about fabric in the next chapter.

These doors feature fluted glass that mutes the objects inside while reflecting light around the room.

of your cupboards to the world (see the photo above). For safety reasons, glass used anywhere in the home should be designed to break into very small fragments or to be relatively unbreakable like laminated glass, featuring a layer of plastic sandwiched between the glass. Any old plate glass represents a safety problem, especially in homes with children. Glass is sold and worked by specialized glass fabricators who can show you many choices and help with decision making.

Wall Coverings

Printed and textural wall coverings are popular in kitchens, and the range of choice is truly mind-boggling. Bear in mind when considering wallpaper or vinyl wall covering that it will be exposed to smoke, grease, steam, and other corrosive elements that can cause it to fail or become dingy over time. Choose wall coverings that are

Left: *Choosing colors and matching wall-covering patterns is an important part of the design process.* Above: *Bright blue paint looks crisp against the white of the rest of the kitchen. (Photo above by Carol Bates.)*

easy to clean, and make sure that a professional installs them. Proper installation often includes special wall preparation, use of professional-quality pastes, and close attention to detail to ensure that edges stay down, patterns match, and colors are true.

Overuse of patterned wall coverings, borders, and chair rails (so called because they originally protected walls from chairs) can result in a visually confusing kitchen. A kitchen already has an abundance of color and textural elements, and choosing a neutral solid color for walls often brings out these elements more than a busy paper pattern can.

Paint

Painting may be the last thing done in your kitchen, but it is also usually the unifying element that brings the design scheme together. A quality paint job can make a basic kitchen look great, while a poor job will give a sloppy look to an otherwise stellar design.

Paint comes in water- or latex-based and oil- or alkyd-based finishes. There is a trend toward the exclusive use of water finishes based on environmental considerations. Oil-based paint used to be the preferred finish for kitchens because of its sheen and durability and its ability to be cleaned without compromising those proper-

ties. Today, high-quality latex and acrylic paints have replaced oil-based finishes and offer the same qualities without the special care required to apply them and without obnoxious odors. Always insist that your painter use the highest-quality paint available. Scrimping to save a few dollars per gallon will cost you later when it loses its look and color. Cheap paint often requires more coats, meaning a much higher labor cost.

When choosing paint colors for walls and ceilings, consider them as backdrops for other design elements in your kitchen. Neutral colors can unify a design and help reflect light around a room, while very dark colors can either add drama or suck up a lot of light. Bright white ceilings add a spacious feel to smaller rooms and help distribute light throughout the kitchen (see the photo on p. 147).

Moldings and Trim

Even an architecturally challenged room can be made interesting by the judicious use of quality moldings and door and window trim. On the other hand, overblown fancy chair rails, picture moldings, and crown moldings can turn a simple kitchen into a rococo nightmare. Well-planned trim work installed by a skilled finish carpenter is one of the keys to a successful interior design. Painted trim should be smoothly caulked at all seams by the painter for a clean, finished job. This also gives him a place to paint a clean edge between colors.

Trim surrounds doors and windows, joins ceilings and walls, and may be used to divide and add interest to walls. Crown moldings, chair rails, wainscoting, baseboards, and toe moldings are all options. In choosing them, you should keep historical period and design style in mind. Fancy Victorian molding would be out of place in a '50s ranch, for instance.

Trim can be finished with glossy paints or stained and covered with a clear coat. If you have painted trim and are considering stripping it for a natural finish, bear in mind that if it was painted originally, it is probably a paint-grade wood. This means no attempt was made to match grains or coloring and defects may have been filled with putty. Woodwork meant to be painted probably should be painted. If you are installing naturally finished

The soft green paint in this kitchen matches the tile and brings out the warm color of the wood cabinets and floor. (Photo by Charles Miller.)

Stepped trim is used to accent the separation between the eating area and the kitchen, as well as the great room beyond. (Photo by Steve Culpepper.)

trim, make sure your carpenter matches color, tone, and grain wherever possible and uses clear wood with no knots.

Many moldings now on the market are made from plastics and foams. This is done in part to offset the high cost of solid wood and to mimic plaster moldings with their many fancy de-

tails. Properly installed and painted, they should be indistinguishable from wood. Very cheap plastic moldings may have rounded edges and other inconsistencies that may give away their inexpensive nature.

Every day new material choices and options come onto the market. Re-

searching these choices and creating a palette of materials that appeals to you is the first step in cutting through this bewildering variety and making choices that work. Consider each material's maintenance, durability, cost, and installation requirements along with its aesthetic appeal before you make your choices.

CHAPTER 12

Furniture and Accessories

The overall design of your kitchen isn't complete until you add those final elements that turn a newly built kitchen into one that is lived in and shows the character of the users. Furnishings, art, displays, textiles, and window treatments all contribute to the ambience of the finished kitchen. A kitchen stripped of these things looks like a display in a store—artificial and lacking in life.

Choosing these elements is a very personal process. For some, a simple collection of the necessary functional tools completes their kitchen, while for others an accumulation of objects and collections in the room makes a connection between the kitchen and the rest of their lives. As a central gathering place, kitchens should have places to post messages, keep calendars, and display a favorite photo or a child's recent drawings. There is often a temptation to try to hide these messy elements and to keep your kitchen's pristine basic design intact. In the real world, most of us cannot and will not keep to a regimen of clearing the space. We like the feeling personal objects give us.

Below: *These finely crafted stools make a simple seating area visually interesting.*

Furniture

Choosing freestanding furniture for a kitchen is an integral part of the design process. These furnishings may be something basic, like a set of stools, or a large piece, like a buffet or commercial butcher-block cutting board (see the photos at right). They often stand out as both functional and visual elements, and by choosing an unusual item, you can create an interesting contrast with the rest of the space. For example, a large antique maple cutting block with its characteristic patina and unusually worn surface can fit in well with an otherwise ultramodern design. The combination of the very tactile and massive block with the sleek finishes of flush cabinetry balances the overall look.

There is a temptation to make coordination the Holy Grail of the design process, with everything matching everything else. This simplistic approach can result in a monochromatic, lifeless room if followed as a rote guideline. A better approach is to choose a range of objects that fit in

with your design palette without necessarily repeating the same motif. For example, your breakfast area might feature wrought-iron chairs with fabric cushions. You might have chosen black iron as a material because of your black-iron cabinet pulls or your collection of cast-iron cookware, rather than because of a hard-and-fast rule that all furnishings must be black.

Furniture for your kitchen should be easy to clean and durable because of the casual atmosphere of the space. Socially, a kitchen is a place to relax informally, as opposed to a more formal space like a dining room. This informality can be extended to furniture chosen for comfort and easy upkeep rather than for high design. If you've created a low-key kitchen designed to work as a backdrop to food and drink, a few radical furniture choices can inject a spirit of fun into the mix.

Decorative Objects

Art should be everywhere in the home, including the kitchen. Even if you only hang a few culinary prints or a favorite photo, art adds color and contributes to a creative atmosphere. Collections of favorite objects, displays of craft items, and visible storage of cookware all add to the overall feeling of the kitchen as a socially interesting and relaxed space (see the photos at right).

Spice and pot racks, jugs of wooden spoons, displays of copper baking molds or antique kitchen tools, and other displays combine visible storage with a decorative element. The kitchen has been a center of focus for some of the finest industrial designers of this century, resulting in tools that are both functional and pleasing to the

Top: *Antique flower prints bring a sense of color and history to the work areas of this eclectic kitchen.* Above left: *A collection of ceramic fish on a shelf of their own adds color and personality to this kitchen.* Right: *This collection of knives has a sculptural quality when displayed.*

Above: *Large overhead racks filled with cookware must have enough room to work beneath them without placing pans out of reach.* Top right: *Well-placed spice racks mounted next to the stove can be easily reached while cooking.* Bottom right: *A custom cabinet for wine storage can also provide visual interest with its grid work and pattern of colored corks.*

eye and hand. Bringing these objects out of hiding solves both storage and design problems.

Pot racks are extremely functional, although they require a dedicated space, structurally sound attachments to ceiling or walls, and room beneath them to work while still keeping them within reach (see the left photo above). Areas over islands and counters work well for the racks, although

rooms with very low ceilings may pose a problem. Wall-mounted racks are one solution. Racks also have a sculptural element and can add a metallic accent to the room. Combined with a battery of attractive commercial cookware, they give a kitchen designed for serious cooking a work-oriented look.

Textiles

It is easy to add color, warmth, and texture to any kitchen by introducing textiles or fabric. Area rugs, woven wall hangings, upholstered seating, and towels and linens are just a few of the places textiles are found in and around a kitchen. Unless fabrics are functional cooking tools like oven mitts, you'll want to locate them in social areas rather than in the food-prep and cleanup areas of the kitchen. You can add swatches of fabric easily by using removable seat pillows and a variety of towels and place mats. More permanent design elements made of textiles include upholstered banquettes or built-in seating areas and fabric wall coverings.

The use of woven materials in a kitchen isn't limited to loomed fabrics. Baskets, jute and straw matting, grasscloth wall coverings, and other natural crude fibers also bring textural elements to the design mix that aren't found in other materials. They are also very practical and inexpensive, meaning a big spill on a jute rug won't be the end of the world. Baskets, in particular, are useful both as storage and as decorative elements, especially when hung in groups on a wall or ceiling or displayed on shelves. Woven shades, sheer curtains, and blinds are other ways that textiles can make a big impact on the overall comfort level and aesthetics of the room.

Window Treatments

The windows in your kitchen are a primary source of light and air, both good reasons for avoiding heavy window treatments or covering them with dark blinds. As a work space, a kitchen requires strong light sources. It also generates smoke and airborne grease, which can make fabric curtains a poor choice. Window-treatment style and materials should be chosen for how well they fit in with your design palette combined with their ease of function. If you must use window treatments, we prefer venetian-style blinds and/or simple sheer curtains that are washable. An unobtrusive

Translucent blinds allow light in without compromising privacy. They also help to reduce glare and heat during summer months. (Photo by Charles Miller.)

blind can be pulled up during the day and closed for privacy at night without compromising the window as a light source. Blinds are available in a wide range of materials and styles. You can get samples to try with your color scheme before you order (see the photo above).

When you choose the furniture and accessories for your kitchen, keep in mind that these elements will reflect your personality and taste and

will give your kitchen much of its character. Using hard-and-fast design guidelines to choose objects limits the overall appeal of the kitchen. Instead, include a few of your favorite things from your old kitchen and integrate them with new purchases like well-designed tools you can display. This is your opportunity to personalize your space.

Part Three

BUILDING YOUR KITCHEN

CHAPTER 13

Construction Scheduling and Contractors

The construction of a new kitchen is both a frightening and an exhilarating experience. Your old kitchen disappears in a few days, and what was once a familiar room becomes an empty shell. Your house is filled daily with workers who start out as strangers and end up being someone you share your coffee with in the morning. The mess and dust is a constant problem until that day when you walk in and a layer of wallboard has magically turned the raw space into a new room.

In earlier chapters, we've looked at how to anticipate and make the many choices that eventually result in a good kitchen design. In this chapter, we're going to look at

This is a kitchen prior to demolition. The only element in this photo to survive the renovation will be the antique butcher block in the foreground (see the photo of the remodeled kitchen on p. 175).

The Master Schedule

Because the relationship between your daily lifestyle and the construction process is so important, you must create an overall master schedule for that process. Your master schedule will cover numerous aspects of the construction process from the planning you're already doing to the final evaluation of the kitchen weeks or months after its completion. While every schedule is subject to unexpected setbacks and even the occasional job that goes faster than expected, just writing out a schedule will help everyone involved keep up. It also gives you a realistic idea of how long the project will take and tells you when you need to take action. The master schedule is also a useful tool for budgeting, showing you when you'll need to make purchases and payments and helping you make many of the decisions necessary to keep things moving toward completion.

Your daily, weekly, and monthly lifestyle during construction will affect your planning. A kitchen or any other major remodeling project should be scheduled when it will have the least impact on your lifestyle. This may mean not letting it overlap with school vacations, visits by guests, periods when you are exceptionally busy, and other times when you need your home as a refuge and place of control. A house under construction is not such a place.

Of course, there are numerous areas where even the most carefully planned project schedule can get behind. Your appliances might be back-

the steps involved in the construction process so you can once again anticipate problems.

This process starts with a master schedule for the construction of your kitchen. The schedule is created before you actually start construction to map out potential problems during construction. Planning the construction stage of your kitchen is just as important as planning your actual design and purchases; it will save you both time and money. Of course, in addition to a well-planned schedule, successful construction requires good workers, so we'll look at how to hire contractors, too.

We'll also give a step-by-step overview of the construction process, from getting the permits required for

the work to moving back into your new kitchen. Developing a clear understanding of how, why, and when things happen throughout construction will help you avoid many costly problems. If you're working with an architect or designer, he'll help throughout the process, from choosing materials to ensuring that work is completed as specified.

The information in this chapter will help you understand how a kitchen is built, while the following chapters will address more specific aspects of the construction process, including how to resolve the various problems and conflicts that can arise.

ordered or arrive in the wrong finish or size. A conflict with a subcontractor might mean finding a new plumber just as work is ready to begin. During demolition, obstructions can show up, creating unexpected delays and expense. These and many other conflicts can wreak havoc with schedules. Experienced planners and builders build in time for unexpected setbacks.

The design process is the one place in the master schedule where you may have unlimited time. Some cooks spend years dreaming about and planning their perfect kitchen before even considering the reality of construction. Others work on a tighter schedule, driven by a pressing need for change.

During the planning stage, if you're working with an architect or designer, he should not only draw up blueprints but also include a comprehensive specifications list detailing what materials are to be used where (see the example on p. 162). The list should include dimensions, brand names, color or finish, and it will be used by the contractors to write their quotes. If you are not using a designer, you will need to prepare this list yourself or with the help of your general contractor.

Hiring a General Contractor

Every project needs a designated general contractor, or GC, to handle scheduling, cost control, hiring and firing of subcontractors, and problem resolution. The GC also keeps the overall plan in mind and ensures that all permits and zoning regulations are adhered to.

When you hire a GC, start by asking suppliers, friends, your designer, and others for recommendations. Look for someone who has extensive experience with kitchens and who is not dedicated to always doing them a certain way. One of the biggest challenges in finding a GC is getting one who understands and follows your vision. Often the GC has built many kitchens of similar design and is only comfortable doing what he knows. Be especially aware of an arrogant or inflexible attitude at this stage, as it will mean problems later.

Once you have some names, meet with each GC and ask them for names of previous clients, what their availability is, and how they go about the construction process. Call every reference they have and talk to the homeowners they have worked with, asking about problems and resolutions, as well as their overall experience. Some homeowners may let you see the work. If that's the case, look at the job critically for fit, finish, and attention to detail, as well as the design problems they faced. If a job is very different than your own, look for a more similar one.

Ask your candidates for professional and financial references and for proof of insurance coverage for both injury and liability, and check everything. If they use a materials supplier like a lumberyard as a reference, call and ask about their creditworthiness. It may seem nosy, but you don't want them to have problems getting your materials because they have unpaid bills. Don't skip these steps—you'll be entrusting this person or company with large sums of money and the security of your home for weeks or months.

Once you've narrowed your search for a GC down to two or three choices, you have to decide whether you're willing to pay for quotes. If you have a complete plan and list of specifications, you can reasonably expect a GC to provide you with a free quote. If your plans or specifications are incomplete, you'll be asking them to fill in the blanks and should expect to pay them for their time and knowledge. It is a good idea to let the contractors know you are getting multiple quotes, as it may help keep them competitive in their thinking.

GETTING ESTIMATES AND SIGNING CONTRACTS

Pricing all the elements of a project like a kitchen can be complex. Each quote you receive should be on a standard printed form specifying price, terms of payment, what exactly is being done, who supplies what materials, and when the work will be performed. The quote should also provide for a method of resolving conflicts as covered in Chapter 15.

At the beginning of the process, much of the pricing will be estimates, made in good faith but not accurate to a specific, final amount. Use these estimates for planning, and when you have chosen the GC you want to work with, have him prepare a specific

SAMPLE SPECIFICATIONS LIST

March 27, 1996

Kitchen Design Associates

- Remove existing kitchen cabinetry, appliances, counters, flooring, and ceilings.

- Widen opening to rear area by installing new header to be buried inside of ceiling, attempting to maintain the existing ceiling height of 100 in.

- Build wall at staircase.

- Close in existing archway into dining room and open new archway as shown on plan. No door to be included at this time.

- Relocate plumbing for sink and refrigerator. Provide gas line for cooktop.

- Install electric wiring required for new kitchen, including outlets and switches. Provide and install 9 new recessed can lights with white trims. Provide box for pendant fixture over breakfast nook. Provide and install 5 undercabinet "inch" lights. Relocate telephone.

- Drywall new partitions and ceiling.

- Trim to match existing, including new archway into dining room. Add paneling to match in eating area. Replace bottom 2 treads on stairs with 2 finished side treads. Build bench in eating area with cherry veneer paneling. Tops will be hinged for access. Stain to match cabinetry. Install crown molding around room ready for paint.

- Install cabinetry and associated trim as per plan.

- Supply and install plastic-laminate countertops, including breakfast bar.

- Install tile backsplash—tile provided by owner.

- Provide and install prefinished ¾-in. by 2½-in. oak flooring throughout the kitchen and eating area. Provide threshold at new dining room arch and foyer. Refinish existing stair treads.

- Paint walls and ceilings. Paint two walls of dining room to match existing.

- Remove all debris from job site.

quote. Most standard quote formats are signed by the contractor and provide a place for your approval. Once you've worked out the details, write in any changes, have the contractor initial them with a date, and sign the quote yourself. The quote now becomes a contract binding both parties. Usually you'll make a deposit to get the job started, and work will begin.

The terms of payment are usually based on meeting various goals or stages in the process. The contract may start with a good-faith deposit of one-quarter or one-third of the total. A second payment may occur upon completion of the next stage, continuing until the project is complete. It is common to hold back 5% to 10% of the total until after the entire job is complete to ensure that any final repairs or punch-list items get completed (see p. 174).

Your GC may be required in your contract to hold funds in escrow to cover any subcontractors taking off with your money or not completing a job properly. In lower-budget jobs, this is less of a risk, but large and expensive kitchens can involve enough money to consider having your contract approved by an attorney familiar with construction. Most of the time you can and should work it out with the GC yourself. If you have a construction loan from a bank for the project, it will only disperse funds upon completion of various stages after an inspection. You should be equally careful with your own money.

Once you have quotes, consider more than price in making your decision. How do you feel about working with this person? The two of you must share a vision for a long project and be able to resolve the inevitable problems and conflicts that will come. Do you share the same concerns? Does the GC offer insight into the design problems you've been working to solve? Will he or she get the project started and finished on schedule? These things may require you to trust instinct more than facts, but if you've done your homework, you'll have a good idea who you want to work with by this point.

Price, while important, is not everything. A very low quote may mean that the GC is either inexperienced or plans on hiking his costs after you're deep into the project. A very high quote might mean he's taken measure of your resources and decided you can afford to pay more. Getting three quotes, while labor intensive and potentially costly, will immediately tell you if one or more candidates are out of the ballpark. All things considered, look for quality and reliability over price as criteria for choosing your GC.

SUBCONTRACTORS

Your GC will use many subcontractors, or subs, on the job unless he's part of a large company with specialists on the payroll. Subcontractors are specialized workers like electricians, plumbers, drywall installers, and others who come in at one or more stages of the construction process to complete one part of the project. Their work is often dependent on the work of other subcontractors, and a delay by one can stop an entire project. Specialized materials like large appliances, cabinetry, and lighting fixtures will need to be on-site when the subcontractors responsible for their installation are scheduled. Keeping all of these elements organized requires good contracting skills and access to quality, dependable subcontractors—an important consideration when choosing your GC.

GENERAL LABORERS

Your GC and the subcontractors will use helpers, assistants, apprentices, and other laborers for many of the less-skilled tasks. Make sure they are properly supervised and not trusted with jobs beyond their abilities, but remember that many of these assistants are quite experienced. If you have questions about their work or behavior, go to the GC for answers rather than trying to supervise them yourself.

The workers on your project are likely to be skilled people who like to do good work when given the opportunity. You, as the homeowner, can help create or destroy the environment that makes a good job possible. Too much oversight, rudeness, looking down on the workers, or criticizing them publicly to their bosses is a sure way to get a lousy job. Treat everyone on the job with respect, get to know their names, keep a coffeepot or cold drinks handy, and praise their work, and you'll have a good experience. You don't have to pour it on, just treat them like normal, intelligent, and sensitive human beings, and the whole experience of having people working in your home will be a good one.

One of the first steps in demolition is covering all doorways with dust barriers to prevent dust and dirt from spreading through the house.

The Construction Process Step-by-Step

Once you've found a good contractor, you should spend time with him and your designer planning your master schedule. Their experience will make the process much clearer and easier because they have a good idea of what's involved. To help you better understand the process, let's look at each of these steps in more detail.

Before we begin, though, a note about time and scheduling: Providing a time frame for each of these steps is difficult because it varies greatly depending on the size and scope of the project. A kitchen in a new house may progress much faster than a historical renovation for instance. Creating a schedule specific to your project is part of the estimating stage. Your GC should be able to give you a reasonably accurate completion date. To avoid delays you may want to consider putting a financial incentive into the deal for completing work on schedule. It's important to remember that any construction project can be held up by unexpected problems. However, good planning will keep them to a minimum.

PERMITS AND INSPECTIONS

Either you or your GC must apply for any municipal permits for the construction. These permit applications may result in unexpected complications, particularly if you are remodeling a historic house, adding on to the structure, or making significant internal structural changes. You may have to have inspections done before, during, and after construction, appear at hearings or before zoning boards, or

Acting As Your Own General Contractor

You may be considering acting as your own GC. The main reason for doing the job yourself usually comes down to money. GCs get paid well for their work, often a percentage of the overall job cost, and if things are tight, their fees often make tempting targets for cost cutting. But unless you are very experienced in all aspects of construction, are available around the clock, and have extensive resources, you're probably not going to save anything. Your inexperience will cause delays, you'll pay too much for everything from labor to materials, and you won't have enough pull with the subcontractors when problems arise.

If you are experienced and have the time, carefully consider the value of your time before choosing to act as GC. Is your time more valuable doing the work you normally do? It doesn't make sense to walk away from the work you do best to take on a project you're only slightly familiar with. You should also consider the value of maintaining an arms-length relationship with the workers involved. You have more power when you're paying the bills than when you're in the trenches sharing the dust and dirt.

If you do decide to act as the GC, then start educating yourself now. There are numerous books on contracting that you should read. Start interviewing and seeking out qualified subcontractors. Be sure to check their schedules, as they may be booked for months ahead and scheduling around their availability is a major part of contracting. Decide now what you will do yourself and what you will hire out. Set aside a lot of time for planning, phone calls, trips to suppliers, and dealing with subcontractors. It is a lot of hard work.

even change your plans at the last minute. Inspections and permits involving utility contractors like plumbers and electricians are often arranged by those subcontractors. Determine who is responsible for these items before signing any contracts.

ORDERING

Once you have your budget established and your permits in hand, you'll need to order materials, appliances, cabinetry, and various items like lighting fixtures and fans. As you order each item, make sure it's currently available and in stock at the distributor. Purchasing will be covered in greater detail in Chapter 14.

HIRING SUBCONTRACTORS

Generally subcontractors are hired by the GC based on his previous experience with them. Your GC also represents an ongoing source of work to the subcontractors, which may make hiring them easier. If you are hiring the subcontractors, you may not have as much clout because you are viewed as a one-time job. And you probably won't have worked with them before to know their reputations.

DEMOLITION

Demolition is the first stage of a remodeling job or renovation. If you are building a new home, you won't go through this step, but you may be dealing with related aspects such as waste removal and cleanup. In most cases, demolition won't take longer than a week unless you are undertaking a large-scale or historical project, which can require care when some things are demolished and others are

After the cabinets are removed, demolition begins with tearing out old plaster and lath.

CREATING TEMPORARY KITCHENS

The length of the construction process can mean going without your kitchen for a long time. Even the most inveterate restaurant-goers will eventually crave a quiet meal in their own home. The lack of a working kitchen is a cause of much of the stress involved in any kitchen project.

If possible, arrange with your general contractor to help set up a temporary kitchen somewhere in your home, perhaps a basement or spare room. It may only involve a table, a microwave, and your old refrigerator plugged into a wall outlet, but that will be enough to prepare the occasional meal at home and coffee in the morning. Be sure to locate any temporary kitchen set-ups away from the construction area with its noise and dust. Scheduling a kitchen project during the summer months is often a good choice because you have the ability to cook and eat outside.

Even a small project can produce large quantities of rubbish.

It's important to clarify what dust-protection steps will be taken by the GC before demolition starts. Use of dust barriers, efficient cleanup procedures, protection of floors and furniture, and the state the job site will left in at the end of each day should be decided ahead of time. These factors should be spelled out in the construction contract. All workers must wear protective gear, including respirators, helmets, gloves, and eye protection. Injuries will halt progress and may involve liability. Make sure that your GC carries adequate insurance or that you are covered on your own policies.

FRAMING CARPENTRY

After demolition, your carpenter will begin rough construction, or framing. This may mean building a few walls or an entire addition. It can mean making significant changes to the entire load-bearing frame of your home to increase space or to create new openings. Materials used include lumber and plywood, and the time will vary from a few days to several weeks. Most other work must wait for the completion of framing although a plumber or HVAC installer may come in during framing to install items buried in walls, which the carpenter will then frame around.

saved. The most important considerations during demolition are safety, arranging for immediate storage and removal of debris, and protection for the rest of the dwelling from dust and dirt (see the photo on p. 164). It is incredible how much dust is involved in tearing down even one wall or ceiling, especially in older homes. You'll need a dumpster or a dump truck for debris removal, and there will be landfill or trash-removal fees.

You may be tempted to take on this aspect of the job yourself. Remember that while it may not take a lot of skill to tear out a room, it does require strength, and you'll be dealing with a big mess. It's hard, dirty work that you'll want to get finished quickly. You should also consider that you'll be running into existing wiring and plumbing (see the photo at right) and that there may be architectural details you want to save—both situations requiring care and skill.

During demolition, waste pipes and wiring are revealed, often requiring special framing or relocation.

Your carpenter is responsible for much of the overall success of the project. The rough framing done at this stage serves as the skeleton of the kitchen (see the top photo on the facing page). If this skeleton is built accurately, many of the next steps, including systems installation, walls, and trim, will be much easier. If it is poorly constructed, out of plumb, or built of inferior materials, the other subcontractors will spend extra time trying to work around its deficiencies, and the overall job quality will suffer.

ROUGHING-IN SYSTEMS

During and after framing, the various subcontractors will come in and do the systems rough-in. This means installing ventilation for heating and cooling; running electrical circuits in walls; running in plumbing supply, drain piping, and gas lines; and installing any other items that will be hidden by walls (see the bottom photo at right). Each of these subcontractors' work may require on-site inspections by municipal authorities before you can close the walls, ceilings, and floors. Don't skip the inspection because in most areas the authorities can and will require you to tear out walls again to inspect if you've gone ahead and closed them up.

It's important to understand that the systems rough-in is only the first step for these subcontractors. For instance, rough-in wiring often means simply running cable to boxes without actually wiring in receptacles or switches. The subcontractors will be back later in the schedule to complete their work. The HVAC installer will complete most of his work during the framing stage, but he may return to install covers, thermostats, or radiators after floors and cabinetry are in. You may also need him to install range hoods that vent outside. During the open-wall stage you may want to bring in other specialists like alarm and audio-video system installers.

The rough framing of a new wall begins the reconstruction process.

Sometimes it is necessary to cut access holes to reach systems that are being worked on. The opening will be covered later.

CLOSING THE WALLS

Once utilities are roughed in, drywall-hanging crews, or plasterers, will come in and cover the walls. This is often an exciting turning point for your kitchen project because it seems like real progress is being made as the new shape of the room unfolds. The once dark, bare wood walls also reflect light when covered with wallboard, and you can start to imagine getting your kitchen back.

Usually other work halts while drywall is hung and finished because the workers need access to the entire space and generate a lot of debris and dust. The process takes several days for an average-size kitchen because it involves hanging wallboard and then applying three or more coats of joint compound or plaster, which must dry between coats. With a drywall job, there is a final sanding and cleanup, and then the walls are ready for paint. Plaster walls get a final smooth coat that does not require sanding, relying instead on the skill of the craftsperson for its final finish.

Once the walls are closed, the overall room begins to take shape. Painting is often completed before cabinetry is installed to avoid painting around cabinets.

Before the walls are closed and the floors are finished, the construction area should be cleaned.

FINISHING WALLS, CEILINGS, AND FLOORS

Once the wallboard is installed, the final finished surfaces of the ceilings and floors will depend to a great degree on the materials being used. Most ceilings will be made of the same material as the walls and will get finished at the same pace. Exceptions include suspended ceilings in which it is common to hang the framing so that ceiling light fixtures and vents can be installed prior to the installation of the finished ceiling. Suspended ceiling panels are usually one of the last items put in place to protect them from damage. Other ceiling materials such as tin panels or wood are installed after wallboard is hung and finished with the walls.

The painters often come in at this stage to do basic wall priming, waiting for trim work to be completed before applying final coats. Ceilings are painted first to avoid splattering paint on walls and floors. Then floor underlayment and sometimes flooring is installed (see the bottom photo at right).

These doorways are being prepared for trim. The opening on the right is new and was relocated to provide better access to a dining room adjacent to the new kitchen.

Crown molding is installed where walls meet ceilings. Here, the painter has carefully caulked all seams in preparation for priming.

Installation of this wood-strip floor takes place before cabinets are set in place. The sanding and finishing are done after the rest of the kitchen is complete.

This is a view of the kitchen shown on p. 160 midway through the reconstruction process.

If finished flooring runs under cabinetry, it is installed now and should be covered with construction paper or drop clothes until the job is completed. Tile, prefinished wood, or man-made flooring is usually one of the last items to be installed to avoid damage during construction.

INSTALLING CABINETRY, WORK SURFACES, AND BACKSPLASHES

Upper cabinets are installed first. They are screwed to the wall after a level reference line is created (see the top right photo on the facing page). Lower cabinets are set in place and leveled

and then screwed to the wall (see the bottom photos on the facing page). Doors are hung and adjusted along with drawers and any on-site installations of inserts or shelves. Counters are either brought in and installed or fabricated in place. Backsplashes are installed, and then everything is caulked or trimmed out to provide a seamless contact with walls and floors. This may involve the installation of custom moldings and panels by your finish carpenter.

This area, which will be the sink and cleanup area, is now ready for the installation of cabinetry.

Upper cabinetry is leveled and securely screwed to wall framing before the installation of lower cabinets.

For these lower cabinets, the base is built on-site and then leveled to make it ready for cabinets.

Lower cabinets are installed on the base and screwed to the walls. The open space at left is for the dishwasher.

This overhead cabinet hangs from supports on the ceiling over a peninsula area. The unfinished end of the cabinet will get a finished end panel that matches the doors. Details like this help bring the kitchen design together.

Undercabinet lighting and all other electrical work is now complete, including installation of receptacles, switches, and trim.

COMPLETING ELECTRICAL, PLUMBING, AND UTILITY WORK

Utility contractors usually return once cabinetry and work surfaces are in place to complete wiring, plumbing, and heating and to test all work. They install outlets and switches, lighting fixtures, ventilation covers, faucets, and any other final controls or wiring. Final inspections are done and approvals issued, which, particularly with new construction, may mean any banks involved will release funds to pay for this work.

INSTALLING APPLIANCES AND SINKS

Appliances are delivered, installed in cabinetry, and hooked up to utilities (see the photo on the facing page). Sinks are installed in counters, drain lines are attached, and faucets are plumbed in and tested. At this stage, the kitchen is functional again, another hallmark calling for celebration.

COMPLETING FINAL TRIM WORK

The finish carpenter comes in and installs doors, moldings, window and door trim, baseboards, flooring, and, working with a punch list (see the facing page), completes much of the detail work.

ADDING FINAL PAINT AND FINISHES

The final steps for painting involve filling and patching holes, caulking all joints, priming any unpainted surfaces, and applying two or more finish coats of paint. Since most of the wall painting is typically completed before installation of cabinetry, this is the time for touch-ups. Once painting is complete, floors may be installed or final floor finish applied.

FINAL DETAILS AND ADJUSTMENTS

Final items include installing cabinet hardware and lighting, such as trim on recessed fixtures, hanging lights, and track lighting. Other common last-minute details include shoe moldings over the joint between the finished floor and the baseboards, the vinyl cove base along the kick area below the cabinetry, undercabinet lighting, pot racks, telephones and audio-visual systems, and any other miscellaneous elements. Cabinet doors and drawers are checked for alignment and proper operation and adjusted if necessary. Cabinet inserts like wire baskets may be installed at this stage and shelves located and installed.

CLEANUP

The kitchen is finally ready for a thorough cleaning, and the debris is removed from the premises. Cleanup also means reading appliance manuals and unpacking appliance accessories and testing them.

PUNCH-LIST COMPLETION

After the schedule is complete, it is common practice for the homeowner and the GC to prepare a punch list of items that need completion and problems that need resolution (see the example on p. 174). These can include anything from dings and dents on a paint job to missing parts for appli-

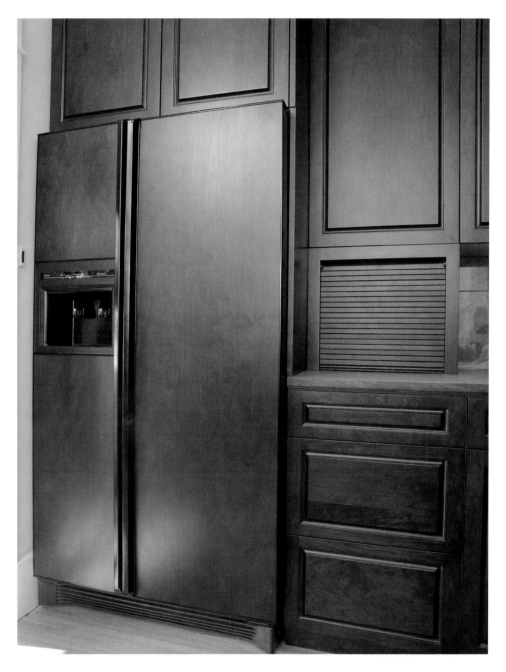

After the refrigerator is installed, it is fitted with panel inserts that match the cabinet finish.

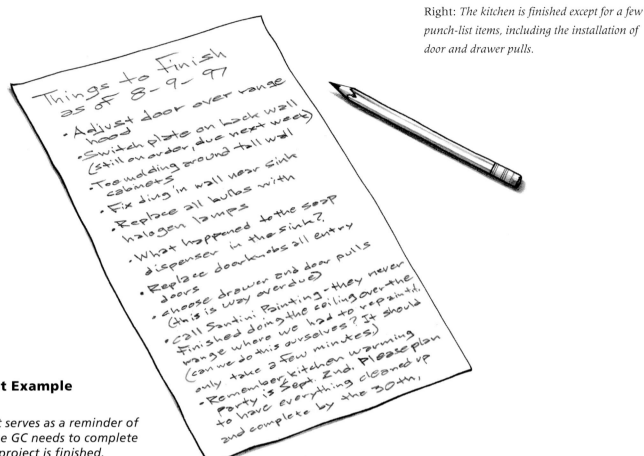

Right: *The kitchen is finished except for a few punch-list items, including the installation of door and drawer pulls.*

Punch-List Example

A punch list serves as a reminder of the tasks the GC needs to complete before the project is finished.

ances and any number of unexpected small details. Until this punch list is completed to the satisfaction of both parties, no final payments are made.

MOVING BACK IN

Last but certainly not least, you'll be moving your kitchen tools and food back in and starting to get organized. Over the first few weeks of use, your design will prove itself and any shortcomings or successes will be obvious. You'll also inevitably find additional punch-list items that you must resolve with your contractor. This step is discussed in more detail in Chapter 16.

Coping with Stress

Everyone is stressed out by the completion of a big project like this. You're tired of having people in your house all the time along with the noise and the mess. The workers want to get the job done, get paid, and get out. Everyone has become very detail conscious, and it is easy to lose track of your original vision. This is normal. In any creative process you start with the general, zero in on the details, and then gradually see the whole reassemble itself again.

Stress can be alleviated if everyone involved remembers that they are all in this together. When someone treats

you with respect, you'll go the extra distance for them. When someone doesn't, you'll be unlikely to put your heart into your work. It's no different with the people you hire to work on your kitchen.

Coping with the flow of materials from initial purchasing decisions to delivery, storage, and waste removal is an integral part of the construction process. In the next chapter, we'll look at how material handling affects the overall success of your kitchen project.

CHAPTER 14

Buying and Handling Construction Materials

In the world that supplies materials for construction projects like your kitchen, there are three choices: materials designed and packaged for do-it-yourselfers, materials designed for the professional contractor and/or designer, and custom-made materials. Sometimes the do-it-yourselfer's material is the exact same item as the professional's material, but it's packaged more attractively or in smaller quantities and the price is marked up. In other cases, the professional-grade material is simply a better product that may not make its way onto the shelves of your neighborhood home center. The custom-made material is often more expensive, but it will be made to fit your kitchen.

Quality lighting, like the track lighting above, and accessories, like the dimmer switches at left, are often more durable and function better than the cheaper versions.

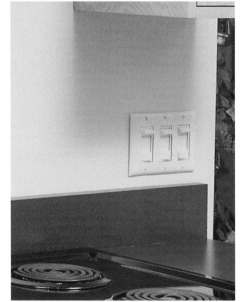

For almost every buying decision you'll make, you'll have at least two choices. Even a seemingly ordinary light switch comes in everything from a cheap 39¢ version to a commercial-grade switch priced five times as much, with several grades in between. The more expensive product is often more durable, quieter, and capable of handling higher levels of current. It may also be safer, although even the cheapest electrical component is required to pass stringent guidelines.

The simple rule for buying construction materials is to always choose quality over economy. Cheap materials will cause many unforeseen problems in the future that can result in expensive disputes, poor function, and shoddy workmanship. Saving a dollar on materials may mean spending several dollars later to fix problems while still not achieving the quality you want now.

In this chapter, we're going to look at how to buy materials for your kitchen. Even if you're not actually buying electrical outlets and dimmers, you may be asked to specify, or spec, the grade you want. And if someone

Trim for recessed lights can be temporarily installed to help you make choices and check out lighting patterns. Having a ready source for these products makes this flexibility possible.

else is doing the buying, you'll still want to know that you're getting the best. Buying the best materials you can afford does not cost you money, it saves you money.

But deciding what materials to purchase is only the beginning. You'll need to plan delivery schedules, storage, and waste removal. So we'll look at how to fit these material-handling issues into your schedule to keep things moving forward.

Suppliers

Today there are two main places to purchase the many different construction materials you'll need: the home center and the professional supplier. Home centers are just that; they offer

almost everything you need for nearly any home project, from complete kitchen-design services to wire nuts. They offer one-stop shopping, low prices on some items (and inflated prices on others), and a good selection. The professional supplier tends to specialize in one area, like plumbing, electrical, lumber, or appliances. The professional supplier's selection is deep in its specialty, and it mainly sells to pros. Although the suppliers may have showrooms for clients of contractors and increasingly sell retail, often they represent extensive catalog lines of items like lighting that are not shown in the average home center.

We have nothing against home centers except that they tend to offer few styles and choices in some items and seem to cater to the budget rather than to the quality buyer. Lumber is

often second-rate, and cabinetry is often what is known as builder grade, made to be used in entry-level new houses. But for small items and generic materials like insulation, they often have sale prices that can't be beat. We recently priced a large quantity of drywall at several places including a wallboard supplier, and a home center beat all of them hands down. The manager explained to us that the price was a loss leader designed to get us in the door.

You may be intimidated by the atmosphere at the wholesale-oriented professional suppliers. But you can get help and answers from their staff if you don't ask at the busiest part of the day, which is usually early morning. To really take advantage of professional suppliers, you need to do your

Granite counters are extremely heavy and can be difficult to maneuver. Make sure they are delivered and installed by experienced workers and measure before ordering to be sure you can get them into the room.

homework before you go in. If you ask for information on manufacturers they carry, you can get catalogs with many options you'll never see in home centers. This is especially true with lighting, plumbing fixtures, and appliances.

Many of the items in your kitchen, including cabinetry, metalwork, stone counters, and furniture, are available as custom-fabricated, one-of-a-kind pieces built by specialized craftspeople. The decision to have a piece custom built can help solve difficult design problems, as well as give you a high-quality product. The downside is the typically higher cost and longer waiting period for these hand-built items. If you decide to purchase custom ma-

terials, you'll need to go directly to the artisan or seek referrals from a designer. When choosing an artisan, you should see his work, get referrals, and negotiate to fit your budget. Custom fabricators can usually be found in the yellow pages under categories like cabinetmakers and metalworkers.

You may also consider used or historic-house parts suppliers as a resource. These businesses buy everything from doors to whole houses scheduled for demolition and sell the parts to renovators and others who want the look and quality only available in older pieces. These suppliers also handle new products such as hardware and heat vents that are ac-

curate historic reproductions. Sometimes a quality older item like a French door lends a patina and sense of continuity to a new kitchen while also offering a cost-effective alternative to new materials. Be aware that using old house parts can add to the labor involved, especially for carpenters and finishers.

Purchasing

Being a knowledgeable consumer means much more than price shopping. You must be concerned with availability, delivery, and storage among other things. Getting a great price on that European cooktop you want means nothing if it is back-ordered for six months.

Often you will be better off having your GC or subcontractors do the purchasing for raw materials like lumber, permanently installed lighting fixtures, drain pipes, and other roughed-in materials. You may not save money, but they will make sure the materials are there when needed, they have the means to transport them to the job site, and they will take responsibility for doing the buying—all major time-savers. You may find a great price for those 200 2x4s you need, but getting them to the site, off the truck, and safely stored away may prove to be a major headache.

A good rule of thumb is to buy the highest quality for anything that will be built into walls or be otherwise permanently affixed to the structure of the house. Items that are easily replaced like appliances may be upgraded in the future, whereas replacing a fixed item like an HVAC system may be very costly. You should also go for the best on anything that gets heavy use like dimmer switches, faucets, flooring, and counter surfaces.

If you have questions about where you can save and where you should splurge, ask your GC or your subcontractors. They may know that a basic recessed light works just as well as its higher-priced counterpart. They may also tell you that a $20 dimmer will be a lot quieter than a $10 one that generates an annoying hum every time it is used. Even if you are buying certain items, ask your designer and GC for suggestions for reputable suppliers.

Your GC can often accomplish more with a few phone calls than you could with hours of research because of his extensive and daily experience pur-

chasing standard building materials. Your time is best spent tracking more exotic items that may not be available at the GC's regular suppliers.

Your contractor can arrange for delivery of the building materials needed for your project.

AVAILABILITY OF MATERIALS

Sometimes your first choice in a material will not be available because lines are discontinued, certain styles are only made on a seasonal basis, or demand has outstripped availability. In these cases, you must remain open to other options if you want to get your project finished. These options include using a different material or supplier or being willing to pay more money for the product. Sometimes if you'll pay the price, those scarce materials suddenly become available.

It is also important not to limit your buying to local suppliers, especially on easily shipped items like lighting, hardware, and even cabinetry. Much Euro-style cabinetry is designed to be

shipped flat and assembled on-site. By looking outside of your area, you may save money or be able to get the material you really want. To find these sources, call the manufacturer and ask who else handles their products or look for resources in design magazines. If you live in a major metropolitan area, there may be a design center featuring showrooms from many manufacturers. It's important to be aware that suppliers are not as familiar with exotic or special-order items. It is critical that you get detailed manufacturers' specifications and go over them carefully with your GC to make sure they fit in your plan and have no unusual supply needs or parts.

DELIVERY SCHEDULES

The arrival of your materials, especially bulky items like lumber and wallboard, should coincide with the need for them. Otherwise, you'll need to provide dry storage, and you may have to haul the same 100 sheets of drywall around several times. If the materials arrive when you're ready, the delivery truck can hoist them directly into the work space through a window or doorway.

There is nothing more frustrating than to have work stop because you forgot or didn't get a necessary material. Your subcontractors have scheduled your job into their busy work schedules, and not being able to work because of supply problems means

Small waste from demolition can be bagged for pickup, but for larger debris you'll need a dumpster.

they lose money, causing ill will. Giving the GC responsibility for material purchasing and delivery scheduling helps avoid this.

STORAGE

If you can't store materials, ask if the supplier can stock them for you until you need them. You may need to pay a fee for this or pay up front for the materials, but this will be worth it if it means instant availability when you need it. Anything you store yourself must be kept dry, especially building materials. In some cases, materials must be acclimated to the environment before being installed. For instance, hardwood flooring must sit in the room for several days before installation to avoid warping, shrinkage, and cracking. It adjusts to the temperature and moisture level of the room.

If the flooring is installed immediately after delivery, you might end up with a ruined floor.

Waste Removal

One of the biggest material problems on any job site is waste cleanup and removal. Even during new construction there is an incredible amount of waste as a result of the cutting and trimming of materials. In a room with many complex angles, for instance, as much as 50% of the wallboard purchased will end up getting thrown away as useless scrap. This occurs because of the way joints must be matched to make them invisible at the finishing stage.

Even a small remodeling job will require either a dumpster on site or a dump truck for waste removal. As de-

Old working appliances can be sold or donated to charity. In both cases, you can usually arrange for pickup. Be sure to remove the doors from refrigerators you leave at the curb so neighborhood children won't get stuck inside.

A clean job site helps the construction go faster.

molition progresses, workers must be able to take the waste out of the house and put it into a container. Piling it outside may not only be illegal and dangerous, but it also means moving it twice—a waste of manpower. Dumpster fees and landfill fees should be included in your budget. There may also be permits required.

If you own an older home, you may run into asbestos during the tearout. It was commonly used for pipe insulation, fireproofing, and siding. Friable asbestos (not hard and solid) is extremely dangerous in microscopic quantities when inhaled. If you think you've discovered asbestos, work must stop immediately and care must be taken not to disturb it at all. You must hire an asbestos-abatement team with special training and equipment to remove or cover the asbestos. If you own an older home, consider having an inspection prior to starting your project. Abatement is expensive, and you'll want to know what is involved before you start demolition.

It is very important to get the demolition stage over with as quickly as possible and to get the waste materials out of the house immediately because the dust and dirt will find its way into every part of your home. All connecting doorways should be sealed with plastic and tape prior to demolition,

Check your actual costs against your budget frequently to ensure that you don't have any surprises when the project is finished.

and a ventilation source to the outside should be provided to vent dust out and air in. We suggest planning carefully so all demolition can be done at once and then thoroughly cleaning and vacuuming afterwards. A clean work site will mean much faster progress.

Budgeting Materials and Cost Overruns

You won't be far into your project before you find yourself writing checks for hundreds and/or thousands of dollars on a regular basis. It very important to keep a handle on these payouts by keeping an up-to-date budget and questioning any and all unexpected costs or overruns on materials. Budgeting the materials for a complex building project is not an exact science, in spite of all the cost-estimating guides that are available. Give yourself a cushion of 10%, and carefully look at anything that goes far over, checking receipts and counting quantities if something seems way out of line. If there are extra charges not covered in your contract, they must be agreed to by you and by your GC prior to incurring them.

In general, you won't find your contractors out to get you on materials. Instead a bigger problem is the "bump." The bump occurs when you convince yourself to upgrade or add things to your plan in the middle of construction. You're bumping yourself up the next level, and it is an easy way to overspend or run out of money before completing the project. You decide to upgrade a seemingly innocuous

item like a recessed lighting trim that is $15 more than you originally budgeted. Multiply that trim by 12 fixtures, and you just added $180 to your budget. Pick a drawer and door pull that is $7 more, and suddenly you find you've just spent another $250. It is easy in the enthusiasm of seeing your kitchen take shape to get caught up in additional spending. Unfortunately, before you know it you may discover you've spent several thousand dollars more than you planned.

Sometimes the unexpected cost overrun can't be helped. When you open up walls and add to existing systems, you often tax the structure or system beyond the capacity it was designed for. A seemingly small item results in a systemic overhaul. In one job we know of, a radiator needed to be moved several feet over to another location. The plumbing was easily accessed from underneath, and it seemed an easy job. However, when the HVAC contractor came to look at the job, he explained that the system must be drained and cleaned (and upgraded in the process) since it had not been cleaned recently, adding $500 to a small repair. Because cleaning the system was a necessary, albeit unexpected, job, it had to be done.

Damage Control

Having many different workers around and moving large materials in and around your site can mean damage to already completed or existing work and/or materials. Appliance installers scratch newly finished floors, walls get dented, and the occasional lighting fixture gets broken by a ladder

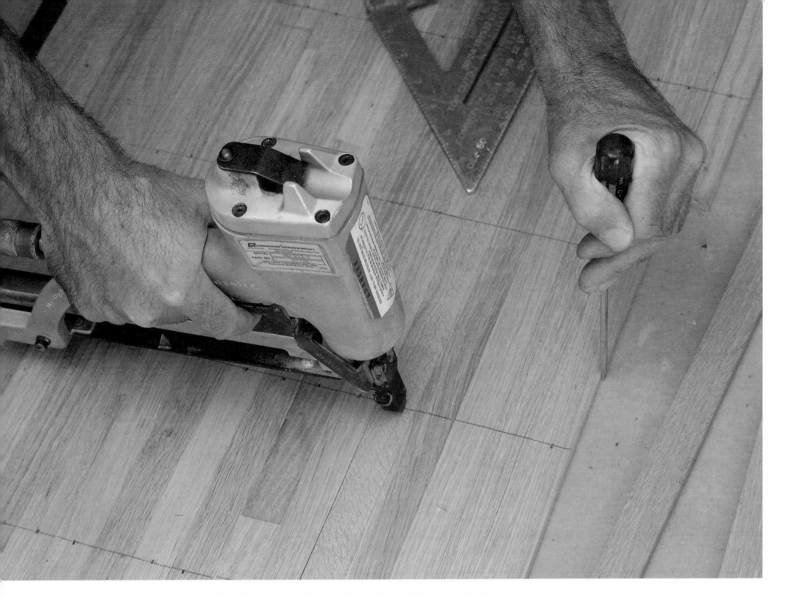

Being organized means allowing each tradesperson the luxury of completing his task efficiently and without interruption. Each material element of your kitchen has to be handled and installed in its own unique way.

or swinging board. These things will happen, and you should prepare for them while taking steps to avoid the possibility.

Make sure your contracts state who is responsible for damage incurred by the actions of workers, and make any claims as soon as you find the damage. Anything shipped or delivered to the job site must be inspected and signed for, with damage claims made while the driver is present. Cover or seal off any areas susceptible to damage, such as floors, adjacent rooms, and outside decks. Don't have final finishing on walls and floors done until all major construction is complete, and carefully supervise appliance delivery and installation if any go in after other workers have left the site. It may be difficult to get someone back for a repair later.

Choosing, buying, and handling the materials needed for a new kitchen requires planning and organization. When you're unsure about a choice, ask the supplier or your GC for advice. Working with contractors who specialize in kitchens will make the process much easier. Things that may seem overwhelming to you may be normal day-to-day experiences for them.

But even the most careful planning cannot eliminate all problems. In the next chapter, we'll look at ways to resolve conflicts and handle unexpected problems.

CHAPTER 15

Problem Resolution

The process of designing, planning, and building something as complex as a kitchen is not an entirely predictable one. No matter how careful you are in your planning, you and your contractors cannot foresee every potential problem, whether it's a bottleneck in the flow of materials or a dispute with a subcontractor. Perhaps the biggest challenge in seeing your kitchen project through to the finish is dealing with the realization that you can't always control the process the way you may be able to control other aspects of your life. It is a continually evolving situation, and you'll be solving problems from the planning stage until after construction is complete.

As a result, you will run into a variety of problems and conflicts that you'll have to deal with on a daily or weekly basis. Some will be simple, like an on-the-spot decision for a subcontractor or a material substitution. Others can be major problems, like no-shows at critical stages, poor performance, and serious breaches of contract. Each of these problems can be resolved, especially if you understand that there is always a solution out there, even if it requires all your creativity and patience to find it. In this chapter, we're going to look at some common problem areas and suggest ways to work around them or resolve them. We'll start with one of the most important problem-solving skills you can learn: how to make the right choices and decisions.

Decisions, Decisions

Perhaps the hardest aspect of building a kitchen is the sheer number of decisions you'll be asked to make at every stage. The painter needs a final color choice, the electrician is waiting to place the lighting, and the carpenter has three crown molding choices and is pushing for one you're not sure about. And in all likelihood, these decisions are all being put in your lap at 7:30 in the morning when you're sending your kids off to school and heading out the door to work. Multiply the number of decisions by several weeks or months, add in a little stress, and the building process can get very difficult.

To alleviate some of the difficulty, it is important to decide on a method of making choices early in the process,

before the start of construction. In the first two parts of this book, we looked at the many choices you should make during the design stage. However, once the kitchen starts to take shape, some of those choices will need adjusting or changing. That color on a tiny paint chip you matched to an equally small laminate chip two months ago now looks really weird. The subcontractor laying the flooring doesn't seem to know what he's doing. The clerk at the appliance store just called to tell you that your oven came in, but it's not the right size for the opening in your custom-built cabinetry. Each of these situations means making a decision, often on the fly as your workers wait.

A good decision-making strategy involves several ground rules, including the following:

- **Assign the decision making to one person.** Getting everyone on the block's opinion is not a great idea. In the same way you chose someone to act as GC, assign yourself or someone else the final say on design choices, and respect that person's opinion. If you are using a designer or architect, this may be a role for him.
- **Let the experts do their jobs.** If you're being asked to locate light switches, for instance, first check with the electrician for code requirements, and then consider your needs. The experts' input will be valuable as long as you make sure they are not simply picking a choice because it makes their work easier.
- **Have second and third choices on everything.** Some things like paint can always be matched, while other items like appliances may require substitution or going to another resource. Having back-up re-

sources and secondary choices can mean being able to respond to problems easily.

- **Be flexible.** It is not the end of the world if something turns out a little different than your original design due to unexpected obstructions or changes in availability of materials. Flexibility means understanding that you have to change when faced with an insurmountable problem. Don't doggedly stick to a choice just because it is written on your plan.
- **Be firm.** While flexibility is important, so is sticking to your guns when you know what you want. Often suppliers or contractors will try to substitute or do things differently because it is easier or because they screwed up. If that is the case, tell the contractor that you want to stick to the plan. It's okay to occasionally remind everyone who is paying the bills without turning into a tyrant.
- **Negotiate.** Negotiation is a process where two people meet in the middle, rather than in a winner-takes-all confrontation. You'll be negotiating all kinds of things throughout the process. By keeping some negotiating basics in mind, you'll be able to keep everything moving forward. These negotiation tactics are covered in detail on the facing page.
- **Finish things.** The ultimate goal during the construction process is to stay on track and finish the job reasonably close to your target date. It is easy to keep adding tasks, changing specs, and fiddling around with the design. You must keep your nose to the grindstone and get the job finished. We've seen numerous kitchen projects left unfinished for months while someone obsesses over a hardware or cabinet-door decision. Get it done.

When Problems Arise

Murphy's Law might have been originally written about construction projects. Often you're hit by a snag just when things seem to be going well, but rather than panicking, focus on the problem. We've seen people build small things up into major problems simply because they can't leave well enough alone. When a problem becomes apparent to you, check with others to first decide if it really is a problem and if so, start thinking about what decision must be made to move things ahead. Let it work around in your mind and in those of others who are working directly on the site. One key to resolving problems is choosing the next step you'll take and how to take it. As obvious as it may sound, breaking problems down into easily resolved stages is a good model for getting things done. Make a simple decision, take action, and then go on to the next step.

Because of the number of people involved, the solution to many problems is negotiation, either at the planning and estimating stage or during the construction process. If you encounter an obvious attempt by someone to lie to you, rip you off, or cheat, get rid of that person immediately. But if the problem is not an overt attempt to undermine you but rather is the result of uncontrollable circumstance, you'll want to sit down and hammer out a way to deal with it that works for everybody.

There are three important aspects of any negotiation: time, information, and power. Each side in a conflict needs one or more of these things to resolve the dispute. For example, you may control the checkbook, a form of power, but a contractor may control your time, another form of power. An exchange of information may be all that is needed to resolve the problem.

To negotiate, you must first define the problem to the satisfaction of both parties. You may say you don't like the quality of a counter material, while the supplier may respond that you made the original choice. The actual problem may be a combination of the supplier's failure to inform you of potential problems and your failure to make an informed decision.

Once you've identified the problem, someone must make an offer. Digging your heels in until you get everything you want is not an effective negotiating technique unless you are 100% certain you are in the right. (If you

Don't panic if some things appear unfinished or incorrectly done. Check with your GC to see if there's really a problem and make sure he follows up on a solution.

feel this way and aren't willing to compromise, you may terminate the negotiation and go to an arbitrator like small claims court, always a last resort). Your opening offer may simply be to discuss a solution rather than to start throwing around threats. This offer to work it out sets the tone. You've admitted there's a problem and you need a solution, so now you need to try to find one that works for both parties. You may offer to pay for fabrication of a new counter if the supplier will replace the material. You've met in middle ground and kept things moving forward, saving yourself time in the process.

Common Problem Areas

There are certain types of problems common to all design and construction processes. In this section, we'll look at a few of the more common situations you're likely to encounter and suggest ways they can be resolved.

NO-SHOWS AND LATE SHOWS

Workers that don't show up when promised or are chronically late can wreak havoc with your construction scheduling. To avoid this situation, you must set ground rules for communication, stating among other things that you must know ahead of time if there is a problem so you can plan around it. If the subcontractors don't call ahead or explain prior to the time of performance, you can either fire them or tell them that they'll be off the job the next time they don't show without calling. If they are chronically

late without explanation, you will need to sit down with your GC and get to the root of the problem.

When materials don't show up, you may have to find another resource. Having your GC take responsibility for materials means that he must deal with supply problems. This is often the best choice because the GC keeps back-up resources in mind on a regular basis because he is more familiar with this process. Finding another source at the last minute may cost you more but that additional cost must be weighed against the expense of idle workers or stopped progress. It's important to remember that one major advantage of using an experienced GC is his ability to pick up the phone and get what you need in a few minutes. Working on your own might mean spending hours tracking down the same resources.

JOBS DONE POORLY OR WRONG

Poor workmanship and aspects of a job done incorrectly are often the result of miscommunication. You must communicate the level of craftsmanship you expect from your GC and make sure he in turn hires workers who are capable of it. He must communicate an intolerance for sloppy or shoddy work and find replacement sources for poor craftsmanship at his expense. When you inspect someone's work and find problems, you must respect the chain of command involved and go to your GC to resolve the problem.

If you're dealing with the problem directly, ask the worker why he did the job the way he did, and if the explanation doesn't make sense, tell him he must either get it right, or you'll have it done over. You can only do

this if you made it clear from the beginning that you would not tolerate poor craftsmanship. It may be that the worker is in over his head and you need a more skilled contractor. Problems like this can be avoided if you carefully check references and make sure that all the contractors have done a similar level of work previously.

Work that does not meet previously agreed upon specifications is a different matter. Some contractors will patiently listen to your plans and then go ahead and do the job the same way they always have. The only way to deal with this attitude is to insist that the contractor sticks to the plan and to have him redo the job at his own expense. If this situation happens, write out a brief memo explaining exactly what you expect. If the contractor tries to tell you that the work can't be redone or that it's too late, having your wishes in writing can give you the clout to make him redo it.

Problems with work not to spec are often the result of the GC not hiring the right person. We've seen several instances where a cabinetmaker who had never built kitchen cabinets was hired to build custom kitchen cabinets. While the cabinetmakers were skilled craftsmen, they were not familiar with the conventions of kitchen cabinetry, conventions that often dictate how other workers will prepare the way for installation, how manufactured inserts will fit, and how other typical problems faced in a kitchen will be solved. The cabinetmakers built structurally well-made cabinets that did not function well in a kitchen environment. To avoid this problem, find out if the subcontractor has ever worked on a kitchen before you hire him.

MATERIAL SUBSTITUTIONS

Another common problem stemming from a lack of communication and/or an unclear determination of who's in charge is unauthorized material substitutions. You, your designer, or your contractor should specify in writing exactly what materials are to be used with acceptable substitutions where applicable. When you use a designer or architect, his plans should have a complete materials list that specifies exactly what he wants used on all aspects of the job. When a subcontractor reads those plans and does a quote based on those specifications, he is legally agreeing to follow those plans as written. Following this procedure gives you solid recourse if you feel that unauthorized changes are being made. As you may understand after planning your kitchen design, specifying materials is a time-consuming job, requiring a lot of research and legwork. Putting those specifications in writing and including samples like paint chips as guides is a good way to make it clear that you will not accept changes without your permission.

If a material is unavailable or if you run into a problem that requires a change in plans, it must be put in writing in the form of a change order after you and your GC agree on the solution and terms. The change order must include specific instructions, drawings, material specs, and agreements on any extra cost and time involved and must be signed and dated by all involved parties. This document ensures that everyone is clear on what is being changed, why, when, and who is paying what. (See the example of a change order on p. 206.)

This sink and counter were improperly installed in front of a window, cutting off the sill area. A better solution would have been to shorten or replace the window.

MONEY

Money is the root of many of the potential conflicts on the job and is therefore one of the primary reasons for putting everything in writing and getting specific quotes and contracts prior to the start of construction. Don't go into the construction process based on "guesstimates" without establishing limits. If a plumber cannot quote a job, for example, without tearing a wall out, discuss the potential worst-case expense, and if it is out of your budget, seek alternatives. Ask for areas where he can limit how much work he does in order to save money. One example might involve eliminating a second sink in a island to avoid tearing floors up to run drains.

Other money problems include the following:

- **A contractor who underestimated the job.** If you a have a signed contract, this should be the contractor's problem. The reality is that it is your problem as well because it may mean the contractor is surreptitiously looking for ways to cut corners to get back to breaking even. If it is obvious that the job was underbid or is more involved than originally thought, it may be to your ultimate benefit to renegotiate the price to cover the contractor's mistake. We realize this may seem unfair, but it can make a huge difference in the quality of the work and the likelihood that it will get done on time.
- **Cash-flow problems.** Cash flow during a job is necessary to keep things moving forward. On your side, it means having your financial resources in place before signing any contracts. Otherwise, your project will come to a screeching halt as the subcontractors get the word that there are money problems. Be sure to put the money aside and pay promptly.

On the GC's side, poor planning may mean that he runs out of cash to pay wages or materials costs, resulting in another slowdown or stoppage of work. If your GC seems to be having financial problems, you can either hire another GC (possibly losing your deposit), or you can hammer out an agreement that lets you pay suppliers or issue checks on an as-needed basis. Don't dole out chunks of cash for unspecified needs, and consider getting some kind of agreement drawn up by your attorney to specify how large sums will be disbursed.

- **Disagreements about completion of work.** Your contract should clearly delineate what constitutes the completion of any stage of construction when a payment is due. If things change as the project progresses, you and the subcontractor involved should sit down and write out an agreement outlining the changes. The deadlines serve to advance progress and keep projects on track. Don't continually change the rules; if the GC or subcontractor has made a good-faith effort to get the job to the next stage, you may want to pay to avoid the cash-flow problems mentioned previously.

ZONING AND PERMITS

In many areas failure to comply with zoning, permits, and local building codes can mean the shutdown of the project, the stoppage of any funds advanced from loans, and worse, being required to tear out any work done without permits, no matter how legal it is. To put it another way, local authorities can and do make people tear out unauthorized work. Make sure that you, your GC, and your subcontractors are aware of all necessary permits and permissions and that they are applied for and received prior to construction.

If you are requesting a zoning change, you may have to plead your case before a zoning board composed of experts, officials, and fellow citizens, often your neighbors. Make yourself aware of the underlying reasons for the codes and try to tailor your changes to represent an acceptable variation rather than a massive departure from the norm. This may mean making your kitchen addition an extension of your Victorian-style home rather than the deconstructionist post-modern cube you have dreamed of.

Bring experts and support materials to the zoning meeting with you, like your designer or architect, your GC, and any drawings, plans, or models you may have. If you're turned down, ask what changes would be acceptable and try again.

UNEXPECTED ARCHITECTURAL OR SYSTEMS PROBLEMS

As we've seen throughout this book, there is a high potential, especially in older homes or houses with a history of numerous remodeling jobs, for unexpected construction problems. Keep in mind that your contractors are experienced with these problems and expect to run into a few things not foreseen. The solutions are not unusual or difficult in 95% of the situations you will run into. Generally, a solution just means a little extra work, the occasional adjustment to plans, and a little of that extra money we hope you kept in reserve just in case. Buildings and their systems are changeable to a great degree, and your contractors have undoubtedly dealt with worse problems than yours. When faced with an unexpected problem, don't seek to blame someone; instead, look for options to resolve it (see the photos on pp. 194-195).

Punch Lists

Near the end of the project is when most of the small items or detailing jobs are completed. This is where the punch list becomes important. You need to make sure that the GC takes care of all of the items on the punch list before he ends the project. It's difficult to get him to come back later. Make sure you go over the punch list with any subcontractors before they leave the site, because much of the work will involve them.

It's important to take care of these details without getting crazy about them. If everyone is gone and you notice a scratch in the paint in the early morning sun that you didn't notice before, don't panic and call the painter. Just get out the paint and touch it up yourself. Most of the punch-list items will probably be handled by your GC during a once-over day at the end of the job. Check them over with him before agreeing that the job is done.

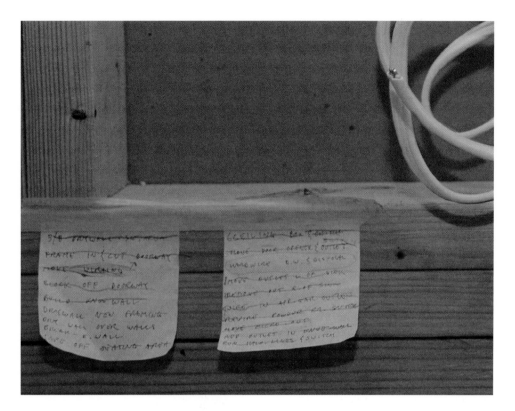

As we mentioned earlier, your ultimate goal is to get the job done. Often this becomes a psychological problem as the project draws to an end and workers leave the site for good. On one hand you're happy to have the house back to yourself, but on the other hand you may experience the letdown that occasionally accompanies the completion of a project. Try not to stretch things out or keep calling people back for small things. Instead, look at what you've accomplished. In the final chapter, we're going to look at putting your kitchen back together for daily use and the ways your new kitchen can and will impact your lifestyle.

You and your contractors should keep to-do lists to track the job. Compare notes regularly to check progress and catch problems before they become significant.

AN EXAMPLE OF PROBLEM RESOLUTION

Even the toughest unexpected problem has its solution. Your contractors know that those solutions are just another step-by-step process. In the photos shown on these two pages, a narrow doorway was expanded to make more space, but a header had to be installed to accommodate the weight of the upper floor, and the pipes needed to be rerouted.

1. The plan called for opening up a doorway in a load-bearing wall. Demolition revealed inadequate framing and hidden drains and wiring from a previous renovation. Both plumbing and wiring, which service upstairs rooms, need to be rerouted and a header built in the new opening to carry the load.

2. Temporary bracing is installed to support the upper floor while the old framing is removed.

3. A new, properly engineered beam is installed to carry the load over the wider and taller new opening.

4. *Additional framing, including support for hanging cabinetry, is installed.*

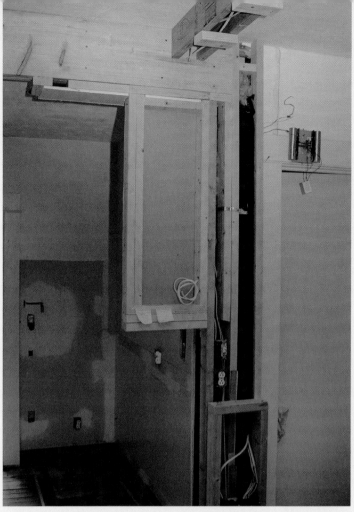

5. *The plumbing and electrical wiring have been moved up and over into the new framing and out of the opening.*

6. *Drywall covers the framing, and the form of the new space begins to emerge.*

7. *The new opening is framed and drywalled. The changes in the construction and wire routing actually helped to open up a previously tight space.*

CHAPTER 16

Working in Your New Kitchen

The last worker has finally left the house, and you've written the last of the checks (you hope). You're standing in your new kitchen—it's clean and you can still smell the newness of the room. You've probably been gradually moving back in as cabinets were installed, appliances were hooked up, and the room was becoming a working space again. Now is the time to stop and consider how you're going to make the most of your kitchen and what you can do to enhance its usefulness.

A brand new kitchen can represent an organizational challenge, but like most challenges it also represents an opportunity. The opportunity in this case is to set up your kitchen the way you've always wanted. You are not going to work the same way in the new kitchen as you did in the old, and there is no reason to automatically put things where they were or even to keep everything from the old kitchen. Part of the reason you designed and built a new work space was to deal with the poor functionality of the old kitchen.

Organizing Your New Kitchen

In Chapter 8, we touched on the organization of your cabinetry based on the way you use your kitchen. The focus was on thinking of areas as work stations dedicated to particular activities like prep work, cooking, and cleanup. You made decisions about what cabinets you needed based on function and then grouped your stor-

age and work surfaces to enhance that particular function. Now, with all your staples, spices, tools, and small appliances out of the room you have an opportunity to really organize your kitchen to fit its new functionality.

Organizing your kitchen should be based on the most efficient way to work rather than on the way you've always done things. Filling a brand new kitchen with all the old junk you've been hauling around since your first apartment just doesn't make

The drawers around the cooktop contain herbs and spices, cookware, and potholders, all within easy reach.

sense. Use this as an opportunity to get the quality tools and ingredients you've wanted and to put them where they'll be used. You'll notice the change in your enjoyment level while working in your new kitchen.

When you organize, we suggest you start by pulling out those old floor-plan sketches and using them to locate where you'd like to put each group of tools and staple cooking ingredients. The groupings might include the following:

- **Cleaning supplies.** Cleaning supplies are usually found under or near the sink and cleanup area. Don't store every bottle of cleaning solution you have under the sink. Choose the ones you use all the time, and either get rid of the others or store them in a safe place elsewhere for special needs. Your new kitchen may require a different level of care than the old one, so if you're never going to use that scouring powder again, get rid of it. It is a good idea to store all these chemicals in a waterproof plastic basin or dishpan within the cabinet to keep any spills from ruining the interior of the cabinet. If you have small children around, be sure to install childproof door catches on any cabinets holding cleaning supplies.
- **Towels and pot holders.** A drawer near the sink is the place for towels, along with carefully placed hooks for dish towels. Go out and splurge and get some new ones that match your kitchen design. Oven mitts and pot holders should be located where they can be quickly grabbed to deal with hot pans. Consider buying restaurant-quality mitts, as they are much safer than the thin kind.

- **Linens.** Table linens should be stored near dining areas.
- **Waste containers and recycling bins.** Waste containers and recycling bins are typically found near the cleanup area. If you haven't already done so, consider using pull-out racks to make these containers easily accessible while hiding them when not in use.
- **Knives and cutting boards.** Knives and cutting boards should be located on or be directly accessible from the work surface between the sink and stove. Knives should always be stored in racks rather than loose in drawers, which is not only dangerous but can dull the blade. Get rid of any old, cheap knives and replace them with a few high-quality chef's knives and a good sharpening steel. The difference between sharp high-quality knives and cheap ones is often what makes cooking fun rather than a chore.

Most kitchens end up with two or three cutting boards, including one for pastries and baking, one for vegetables, and one for meats. Large, heavy cutting boards are difficult to move from sink to counter to stove, which is a common action. Buy quality maple cutting boards because they are better for knives and more hygienic than synthetic ones. They can be stored in a tray cupboard or hung on hooks.
- **Root vegetables.** Onions, garlic, and potatoes must be stored in a cool but not cold place and must have a free flow of air around them. Because they are commonly used in the prep stage of many meals, you'll want to locate them near your prep area in baskets or perforated pull-out drawers.

Everything contributes to the enjoyment of your new kitchen, even the simple tools you take for granted (above) and, as long as the kitchen is well designed, simple tasks like washing and preparing produce (below).

- **Herbs and spices.** First of all, take all those old dried herbs and spices and throw them out. Purchase good-quality new ones and keep them up to date. They only keep their essential flavor and aromatic oils for three to six months. If you've been using old spices, you'll be pleasantly surprised at what a difference fresh ones make. Locate your selection near the stove where it will be close at hand. It's important to know that many dried herbs and spices will only release their full flavor after being cooked briefly, so you'll want them readily available to add during the cooking.

- **Bowls.** The best place for bowls is either in large drawers or on simple shelving that is easy to reach. Ideally, it is better to avoid stacking bowls because it makes getting just one out an inconvenience. If you do have to stack bowls, try to keep those you use most often at the top of the stack.

- **Utensils.** Every kitchen seems to have a junk drawer that catches all those random kitchen tools that everyone accumulates. To avoid the tangled mess that results, start by getting rid of broken and cheap tools, duplicates, and gadgets that don't work. Put the tools you use daily in canisters on the counter where you can quickly grab them during cooking. Put dividers in your drawers and store the less-used tools there.

- **Dishes and tableware.** Storage for dishes and tableware items should be near the cleanup area so they can be easily put away after cleaning. Ideally, this should also be near a dining area to make shorter trips with dishes when setting the table. Trays and serving dishes should be stored closer to cooking areas so they can be easily accessed by the cook. Glassware is often stored in glass-fronted display cabinets, again near cleanup areas.

- **Pots and pans.** Commonly used pots and pans should be easily accessible, either on hanging racks or in pull-out racks in lower cabinets that hold pans and lids without stacking. It's likely that you seldom use more than a few most of the time, so get rid of your lesser-quality pots and pans that you hardly use.

- **Baking tools and ingredients.** Baking sheets and pans can be stored in tall, narrow lower cabinets with special pull-out racks. The baking area may be located between the refrigerator and sink for easy access to dairy ingredients and cleanup. Flours, baking spices, and other dry ingredients should be in the upper cabinets in this area. Mixers and other baking appliances like bread machines may also be found here.

- **Small appliances.** Small appliances should be stored where you use them. This may mean putting the coffeemaker and toaster near a breakfast nook or table rather than in the cooking area. Messy appliances like blenders should be between the refrigerator and sink, while food processors should be near the prep area. Keep those appliances you use daily out and store the rest away in appliance garages or less accessible cabinets (see the top photo on the facing page).

- **Canned goods, cereals, and grains.** If they're packaged, canned goods, cereals, and grains can be stored in upper cabinets or in special

The quality of your kitchen tools enhances the daily experience of using your new kitchen.

pantry inserts that display the contents for easy reference. For loose dry foods like pasta, consider using jars or sealed canisters. Loose grain foods must be stored in airtight containers to avoid infestation.

- **Miscellaneous tools.** It's a good idea to have a small set of tools, including screwdrivers and scissors, that are for kitchen use only. Keep them in an out-of-the-way drawer.

Upgrading Your *Batterie de Cuisine*

Your new kitchen may require you to rethink the way you use your *batterie de cuisine* and may require some upgrades. For example, restaurant-style high-BTU ranges and many new home ranges provide a much higher level of heat than the older appliances you may be used to. Your older lightweight pans may not hold up to these high heat levels.

While we're not suggesting you replace all of your kitchen equipment, you should consider starting to accumulate higher-quality tools to go with your higher-functioning kitchen. It takes a lot of work to create a kitchen that truly works better, and much of your appreciation for your new kitchen will be affected by the tools you use. Along with appliances that function like their commercial counterparts, we've seen many new tools come on the market in recent years that also are of commercial quality.

The difference between high-quality and lower-quality tools is in the construction, weight, and materials used. Heavy tools hold up to repeated use and washings and are built to last forever. Restaurant-style cook-

Appliance garages aren't just for appliances. Here one serves as a minibar that can be easily closed to children.

High-quality cookware distributes heat evenly, lasts a lifetime, and can take the high BTUs generated by commercial ranges.

Besides these very practical considerations, there is a less logical reason for starting to upgrade. The overall feel and look of quality kitchen tools contributes to your enjoyment of your kitchen. These tools are purchases that will continue to be useful for the rest of your life as a cook and will even achieve a patina and grace of their own over time, as will your kitchen.

Maintaining Your Kitchen

Your new kitchen offers a clean beginning from a maintenance viewpoint. Your contractors should have left you with a clean, dust-free environment as part of their completion of the job. There are steps you can take now that will help keep your kitchen pristine and easy to maintain in the future.

Start by taking a few minutes to read over the instructions that came with your new appliances. There have been many changes in appliance technology in recent years, and you shouldn't assume that your new appliances work the same as your old ones. Learn their quirks now and save the manuals for repairs and reference. The manuals will also make recommendations for maintenance and cleaning, including what chemicals should and should not be used for cleaning.

Before turning on ovens, microwaves, and range burners, make sure all packaging and tape have been removed. There may be a "burn-in" period or special instructions for first time use, so read those manuals carefully before firing the appliances up. After the first use of waste disposals,

Preparing a complete meal is a pleasure in a well-designed kitchen.

ware is much heavier, with thick bases made of a sandwich of stainless steel and aluminum that evenly distributes heat, holds up to extreme temperatures, and does not interact with foods the way aluminum can. Nonstick technologies have also seen vast improvements, especially in their ability to resist scratching and hold up to high heat. Very old nonstick pans may actually represent a health hazard and should be discarded.

faucets, and dishwashers, check to make sure all plumbing connections are dry and leak free.

There are often situations where an initial cleaning or polishing is recommended to add an extra layer of protection on new surfaces. Waxing floors before heavy use protects them from day one. Again, check manufacturer's recommendations before proceeding. As we mentioned earlier, don't automatically clean the way you used to. There are many new nonabrasive cleaners, and their use will extend the life of your work surfaces. Areas exposed to hot oils, grease, or acidic liquids like vinegars and lemon juice should be wiped clean immediately, as these can stain or harden and become difficult to remove.

Enjoying Your Kitchen

Perhaps the most interesting change to come about with a new kitchen is how easily you'll forget the old one. During planning and construction, you immerse yourself in the dozens of details, decisions, and problems involved in creating a kitchen. The payback comes when you find yourself enjoying all the activities that take place in your kitchen more than you used to. Kitchen designers know that one of the most gratifying aspects of the work is hearing how peoples' lifestyles change. They renew or start to explore an interest in cooking. They find themselves entertaining more. Their day gets a little less stressful as they leave a comfortable space in the morning and return to one in the evening.

The use and function of a well-designed kitchen should be a major improvement on the previous one. As a result, once-tedious tasks often become much faster and easier, saving time and making the time spent working in the kitchen more enjoyable. Ready access to cookbooks, ingredients, and appliances combined with music or the news on a well-placed TV can mean the difference between meal time being a chore and being a relaxing moment.

It's important to keep in mind that while creating a kitchen that works can be an overwhelming challenge at times, these challenges will be what you remember later on as the best aspects of the process. Identifying and solving design problems in ways that improve on the original is always interesting if you choose to make it so. Often the best kitchens come out of challenging spaces, fixed budgets, or short time frames because these limitations encourage creativity. The real benefit is not short-lived; you'll use your new kitchen every day for many years to come, and the strength of a good design grows over time. Not everything you do may come out perfectly, but like all creative ventures, designing a kitchen is a learning process—one you'll find yourself applying in other areas of your life.

Kitchen-Design Options

	Basic Kitchen	Mid-Level Kitchen	High-End Kitchen
Architecture and Structure	• Maintain the existing architecture • Work with the existing dimensions of the room • Keep existing windows and doors in place • Avoid moving walls • Use quality moldings and trim to enhance space	• Expand into other space in the house • Open up doorways • Move or add windows and skylights • Upgrade existing trim, moldings, and door materials	• Add on to the existing structure • Move or remove major structural obstacles like staircases and chimneys • Move bearing walls • Add large windows, clerestories, skylights • Rework the traffic flow of the house • Expand the volume of the interior spaces • Add outdoor decks, kitchen areas, kitchen gardens
Design	• Work up a plan of space • Comparison-shop for everything • Buy quality rather than quantity • Consider having the basic layout done by a designer • Integrate existing elements and design motifs; don't introduce a whole new design scheme • Where possible, plan to upgrade counters and appliances • Keep traffic-flow patterns simple • Buy inexpensive surfacing materials • Where possible, reuse existing cabinets and appliances	• Talk to several kitchen designers and work with one • Develop an overall plan • Integrate all colors and materials before construction • Choose more natural and more solid surfacing materials • Use cabinet inserts and custom cabinetry • Upgrade to more durable, high-quality appliances	• Use an architect/designer to oversee all aspects of the project • Choose from an unlimited array of materials and finishes • Buy custom-fabricated cabinetry and have it installed by specialists • Buy high-quality commercial appliances
Systems	• Work around existing heating, plumbing, and electrical systems, making changes only where necessary • Add a range of simple but effective lighting • Provide for future upgrades, including space for a dishwasher, wiring for speakers, and additional outlets for small appliances	• Upgrade all utility systems to modern standards • Provide more elaborate plumbing supplies for extra sinks, a dishwasher, ice maker, etc. • Install on-demand hot and cold purified water • Develop a coordinated electrical plan for better lighting and control • Wire for stereo and online needs • Build in general, task, and accent lighting	• Integrate all systems in a whole-house control system incorporating lighting, HVAC, computer and telephones, A/V systems, etc. • Upgrade plumbing, gas, and electrical systems to handle commercial appliances • Install a powerful outside-venting range hood • Develop a high-end custom-lighting plan with numerous control options

Contractor Proposal Form

PROPOSAL

FROM		Proposal No.
		Page No.
		Date

PROPOSAL SUBMITTED TO	WORK TO BE PERFORMED AT
Name _____	Street _____
Street _____	City _____ State _____
City _____ State _____	Date of Plans _____
Telephone _____	Architect _____

We hereby propose to furnish all the materials and perform all the labor necessary for the completion of

_____
_____
_____
_____
_____
_____
_____
_____
_____
_____
_____
_____

All material is guaranteed to be as specified, and the above work to be performed in accordance with the drawings and specifications submitted for above work and completed in a substantial workmanlike manner for the sum of

| Dollars ($). | with payments to be made as follows: |

_____
_____
_____

Any alteration or deviation from above specifications involving extra costs, will be executed only upon written orders, and will become an extra charge over and above the estimate. All agreements contingent upon strikes, accidents or delays beyond our control. Owner to carry fire, tornado and other necessary insurance upon above work. Workmen's Compensation and Public Liability Insurance on above work to be taken out by _____

Respectfully submitted _____

Per _____

NOTE - This proposal may be withdrawn by us if not accepted within _____ days

ACCEPTANCE OF PROPOSAL

The above prices, specifications and conditions are satisfactory and are hereby accepted. You are authorized to do the work as specified. Payment will be made as outlined above.

_____

Accepted _____ Signature _____

Date _____ Signature _____

Change Order Form

Order for Extra Work

No. _____ Owner _____

Place _____ DATE _____ 19 ___

To _____ CONTRACTOR

You are hereby authorized to supply material and labor for extra work

on _____

as follows: _____

_____

_____

For the sum of $ _____ Terms _____

_____ OWNER

ACCEPTED _____ CONTRACTOR

Index

Note: References to illustrations
are printed in italic type.

H

Hardware, for cabinetry, 103
Heating systems:
    as design elements, 79, 80
    electric, 57
    forced-air, 57
    in-floor, 58
    steam or hot-water, 57
    thermostats for, 58
Hidden systems, 52-59
High-end kitchen, 29-30
HVAC. *See* Heating systems. Ventilation
    systems. Air-conditioning.

I

Inspections, permits and, 164-65
Investment, return on, when
    remodeling, 22
Islands, traffic flow around, 41
Isolation areas, 37-38

J

Jobs done wrong, dealing with, 190

K

Kitchen, basic:
    defined, 24
    design choices for, 24-26
        appliances in, 25
        cabinetry in, 25
        current kitchen space in, 25
        floors, walls, and ceilings in, 25
        future upgrades for, 26
        lighting in, 25-26
        planning, 24
        reusing existing cabinetry and
          appliances from, 25
        systems in, 25
        traffic flow around, 26
        windows in, 26
Kitchen, high-end, 29-30
Kitchen, mid-level:
    defined, 26
    design choices for, 26-29
        appliances in, 27-28
        lighting in, 28
        surfaces in, 28
        water, cleanup, and waste removal
          in, 29

Kitchen, modern, evolution of, 8-10
Kitchen technology. *See* Communications
    technology.
Kitchens of the '20s and '30s, described,
    8-9
Kitchens of the '40s and '50s, described, 9
Kitchens of the '60s and '70s, described, 9
Kitchens, pre-1920s, described, 8

L

Laborers, general, work of, described, 163
Laminates, 143-44
Lifestyle design of kitchen, 10-18
    concept, defined, 10
    for the entertaining cook, 16
    for the family, 13-14
    for the serious cook, 15-16
    as a showplace, 18
    as a utility kitchen, 16, 18
    for working couples, 13
Light flow in the kitchen, 40
Lighting:
    accent, 83
    for basic kitchens, 25-26
    general, 80
    for mid-level kitchens, 28
    task, 81-82

M

Maintaining your kitchen, 202-203
Market value of your house, 22
Master schedule, creating, 160-61
Materials:
    assembling a palette of, 136-37
    cost of, 22
    ordering, 165
    substitutions of, 191
    See also specific materials.
MDF (medium-density fiberboard),
    defined, 137
Measuring existing kitchen, 64
Metal, as a material choice, 141-42
Microwave ovens, 90
Mid-level kitchen. *See* kitchen, mid-level.
Models:
    historical, 130-32
    reference,
        discussed, 116-18
        example of, based on favorite
          objects, 124-30

        example of, based on grape arbor
          photo, 118-24
Moldings and trim for the kitchen,
    148-49
Money, resolving problems associated
    with, 192
    See also Budgets.

N

Negotiation tactics, 189-90
No-shows and late shows, dealing
    with, 190

O

Ordering materials, 165
Organizing your new kitchen, 198-201
Outgassing, 40
Ovens. *See* Ranges, ovens, and cooktops.

P

Paint:
    adding final, and finishes, 172-73
    as a material choice, 147-48
Perfect-world kitchen, the:
    discussed, 18-19
    sample list of ideas, 19
Permits:
    and inspections 164-65
    and zoning, 192
Photos, "before," as a design resource,
    70-71
Plumbing:
    completing work on, 172
    supply lines for, 55
    vent lines for, 56-57
    waste lines for, 55-56
Poor workmanship, dealing with, 190
Pot racks, 154
Problem resolution, on paper, example of,
    68-69
Professional design help, 72
    See also Architects. Designers.
Punch lists:
    completion of, 173-74, 193
    example of, *174*

Q

Questionnaire, kitchen design, 11

About the Authors

Martin Edic is a writer and small-business owner. He is an avid cook who has long been fascinated by the subject of kitchen design. His books include *The Woodworker's Marketing Guide* and *Profitable Woodworking,* also from The Taunton Press.

Richard Edic is the owner of a cabinetry and design business in Rochester, N.Y. He has been designing and building kitchens for over 10 years, specializing in custom cabinetry and spatial design tailored to the lifestyles of his clients. He attended the Minneapolis Art Institute as a painter and later took up large-format color photography. As a woodworker, he has done everything from large corporate projects to sculpture fabrication.

Look for other Taunton Press books at your local bookstore or request a free catalog from:

TAUNTON *Direct*
63 South Main Street
P.O. Box 5507
Newtown, CT 06470-5507
(800) 888-8286

Visit our website at www.taunton.com